The [illegible]ow Ghetto Pharmacy

The Cracow Ghetto Pharmacy

TADEUSZ PANKIEWICZ

TRANSLATED FROM THE POLISH BY

HENRY TILLES

HOLOCAUST LIBRARY

An imprint of the

UNITED STATES HOLOCAUST MEMORIAL MUSEUM

WASHINGTON, D.C.

First edition published in Poland, 1947; reprinted in Israel, 1985. This reprint is published by the United States Holocaust Memorial Museum, 100 Raoul Wallenberg Place, SW, Washington, D.C. 20024-2126.

The assertions, arguments, and conclusions contained herein are those of the author. They do not necessarily reflect the opinions of the United States Holocaust Memorial Council or the United States Holocaust Memorial Museum.

Cover photos: *(front, background)* USHMM, courtesy of Instytut Pamieci Narodowej/Institute of National Memory; *(front, foreground)* USHMM, courtesy of Comforty Media Concepts; *(back cover)* USHMM, courtesy of Archiwum Panstwowe w Krakowie

Library of Congress Catalog Card Number: 86-083388
ISBN: 0-89604-087-9

Typeset by Duke & Company, Devon, Pennsylvania
Printed by Victor Graphics, Inc., Crofton, Maryland

Printed in the United States of America

This book is an invaluable contribution to the history of the ghetto in Cracow. The New Cracow Friendship Society in New York, which is composed of a small remnant of Jewish Holocaust survivors from Cracow, is grateful to the author, Tadeusz Pankiewicz, for his objective and independent evaluation of this cruel episode in the lives of the Jews in Cracow during the Nazi occupation of Poland in World War II, as he witnessed it. This story, translated from the original Polish by Mr. Henry Tilles, makes this work accessible to a wide readership and will serve to refute those publications that seek to deny that the Holocaust ever happened.

Roman Weingarten
President,
New Cracow Friendship Society, Inc.

CONTENTS

AUTHOR'S PREFACE

From the moment of the creation of the "Jewish Quarter," I unexpectedly became an inhabitant as the owner of the pharmacy, "Under the Eagle," on Plac Zgody (Peace Square). This was the only one of the four pharmacies in Podgorze located in the ghetto, a circumstance which initially escaped the attention of the German authorities. Later the Germans tried to remove me from the ghetto and offered me one of the formerly Jewish-owned pharmacies in Cracow.

I did everything in my power to prevent this. I resorted to all the infallible methods of bribery. I felt certain, of course, that the Germans were going to lose the war. If I accepted their offer, my pharmacy in the ghetto would be ruined by them, and I would be compelled to return the property to its rightful owner or his family after the war. My fears were justified. My pharmacy would share the common fate of any business or apartment in the ghetto during its liquidation—which meant that it would be completely destroyed.

By a fluke of fate, and through my delaying tactics, I managed to endure in my tragic neighborhood for two-and-one-half years.

For valid reasons, after the liquidation of the "Jewish Quarter," I wrote down my recollections of those unforgettable times and terrible events.

During the entire existence of the ghetto, I was frequently urged by the inhabitants to chronicle its history, since I was the only Pole who, without interruption, lived and worked there until its ultimate liquidation. From the vantage point of the window of the night duty room, I could look out on the Plac Zgody. I saw the most horrendous crimes committed against the Jewish population by the "Occupier."

I have scrupulously verified all of the incidents that I did not witness personally, and I have tried to set them down as authentically as possible.

When I wrote these recollections, I was interested mainly in relating the important events and in remembering the moods and feelings of a once vital community in that dark era of unbearable cruelty.

PREFACE TO THE SECOND EDITION

Almost forty years have passed since the first publication of *The Cracow Ghetto Pharmacy* (Apteka W Getcie Krakowskim). I was frequently asked why there is no new edition of a book that sold out so quickly. Letters were received from abroad. I suffered occasional unpleasantries from "certain compatriots," who suspected me of favoring the Zionists and adversely appraised my activities and the duties I performed during the nightmarish days and nights of Nazi occupation.

My friends often insisted that I publish a complete memoir of my work during that time at the pharmacy "Under the Eagle" (Pod Orlem). The first edition, for various reasons, appeared to be somewhat incomplete. The present enlarged edition is not identical with the first. It contains the whole of the first edition with many additions and several new segments.

Today, from the historical perspective after so many years, while glancing over the pages of my manuscript, the events, scenarios, and problems graphically return to life. I vividly see in my mind's eye the figures who moved through the pharmacy. I wonder how many of them have passed on. How many escapees have emigrated to all parts of the world?

Availing myself of many invitations, I traveled to numerous countries. In 1957 I spent three months in Israel. In 1965, I was invited to New York. There I participated in and spoke at many meetings which were arranged by Polish Jews. I was able to compare their experiences and reports with my memories. I met old acquaintances from the ghetto at various court proceedings against war criminals in West Germany, where I appeared as a witness along with these friends.

My memoirs are not ambitious enough to be considered an eyewitness historical treatise; however, they can be a contribution to the records of the occupation and of Polish and Jewish martyrdom. They are true reports, trustworthy, written while they were still etched in my memory, immediately after the conclusion of the war when I was still haunted by the fresh reflections in my mind of all the events, causes, and the people involved. I was also able to use many of my random notes made during the occupation.

I also fervently desired to commemorate this epoch in the Cracow ghetto, which was a nightmare not only for the Jews but also for my coworkers and me. They helped as much as possible, and often saved the lives of those condemned to extermination.

The climate in the ghetto was so peculiar, so unusual that it is virtually impossible to describe how the people really felt and what they thought, these shadows who dwelt in this "inferno." *Cracow Ghetto Pharmacy* could, in my opinion, throw additional light on the mechanism of attitudes and the behavior of people in danger, fear and dread at impending perdition. The attitudes of those who were the perpetrators of these abominations could contribute to the comprehension of the psychology of the criminal and his victim.

I did not attempt in my reporting to comment on my personal experiences. I did not strive for even a hint of synthesizing. I tried in a most faithful, perhaps even naive manner to describe what I actually saw. This perhaps may sometimes account for some digression.

The present edition is not only expanded, but it is enhanced with photographs and reproductions which are reflective of the time.

I wish to thank my friends, particularly Mgr.[1] Fryderyk Nedela and Dr. Jozef Wronski, for their efforts in my behalf, to implement the publication of this work.

Tadeusz Pankiewicz

1. Magester or Master of Pharmacology

FOREWORD

The pharmacy operated by Tadeusz Pankiewicz was located on the corner of Peace Square in the district of Podgorze in the city of Cracow. Peace Square happened to be in the area which the SS walled in and designated as a Jewish ghetto. Mgr. Pankiewicz was the only non-Jewish Pole permitted to remain inside that ghetto.

This is the story of his heroic endeavors to subvert the intentions of the SS towards the Jewish population of the ghetto. It is an astonishing tale of the barbarities Pankiewicz observed and recorded, of the heroic mercy he extended to his fellow Poles in the ghetto in general, and in that narrow square, which served the SS as a marshalling yard from which Polish Jews made—so many of them—their last journey.

Some years ago I researched and wrote a book about a heroic German, Oskar Schindler, whose destiny was also very much involved with the rescue of Jews from Cracow. Amongst all the survivors I interviewed, the name of Pankiewicz shone. I am delighted that now his name will shine before a wider audience, before the people who encounter this remarkable book.

Thomas Keneally

The author in his pharmacy with one of his assistants

CHAPTER 1

CREATION AND ORGANIZATION OF THE GHETTO— NEW LIFE, NEW FRIENDS

In the beginning of the year 1941, there was frequent talk about a ghetto that was to be created; various locations were mentioned. There were many conjectures on this subject. The rumor most often heard was that Kazimierz would become the future Jewish town because it housed the largest Jewish concentration and was rich in historical tradition. Some thought that the Grego'rzki, a quarter located on the Vistula River, would surely be selected because the Vistula, which formed a natural boundary on one side, would shorten the breadth of the enclosure . . . economy first.

On the third of March 1941, the regulation regarding the creation of the so-called "Judischer Wohnbezirk" or "Jewish Living Quarter" issued by Wachter, Governor of the Cracow Region, was published in the *Krakauer Zeitung*. Its choice was motivated by hygienic and security reasons. Its area was defined in the district of Podgorze on the other side of the Vistula and beyond a boundary line which was to separate the ghetto from the Aryan section.

March 20, 1941, was designated as the deadline for all "Aryans" to leave the areas planned for the ghetto, and the Jews from Cracow (of a total of 80,000 there were 15,000 left) were to occupy their apartments.

People were utterly amazed. Everyone who was directly involved did not want to believe that this was a definite decision. Delegations were organized, composed of citizens of Podgorze who were immediately affected. Meetings were called, appeals and applications were prepared consisting of all kinds of objections such as the number and type of various larger and smaller industrial buildings and mechanical workshops, which could not be transported because of lack of suitable accommodations, etc.

Among others, the vicar of the St. Joseph Parish, Rev. Jozef Niemezynski, offered to intercede; first personally and directly and also through the bishopric. Creation of the ghetto in the boundaries prescribed in the *Krakauer Zeitung* adversely affected the interests of the Parish of Podgorze most directly by depriving it of the majority of the faithful who would have to move to the other side of the Vistula.

Besides, access to the church would become very difficult for many parishioners. In order to reach it from the streets located southeast of the ghetto, such as Wielicka, Zablocie, and Plaszowska, one would have to go around the entire ghetto, adding a considerable distance to the trip.

All the intercessions, delegations, petitions, and appeals were of no avail. The stock German answer was: "In Cracow there are too many churches. Be happy that the church was not located within the walls of the ghetto, because if it were, all the faithful from the Parish would be lost." The decision of the German authorities was immutable: establishment of the ghetto in the area defined by the occupier and at the time designated HAD TO BE CARRIED OUT.

The wanderings began. From daybreak until late at night, platforms, furniture vans, farm wagons, and pushcarts were dragged through the city streets, carrying the possessions to the new habitations. The rush was incredible because the time was short and the desire to obtain suitable apartments was urgent.

One day was like another: the same complaints, the same rush, the same noise, lamentations, and crying. People fainted from exhaustion. Some carried their belongings on pushcarts alone, often from remote streets. The face of Kazimierz was changing every day. Its character, built up through the centuries, was rapidly disappearing. Families who had settled in the quarter for hundreds of years were leaving, and shops were closing, as well as restaurants and synagogues on which the passage of time had left their mark. The typical original sights were disappearing from the streets of old Kazimierz. There were no Jews dressed in long black capotes and felt hats, skull caps and fur hats or wearing beards and long sideburns; gone were the discussions on the street corners and plazas, with characteristic gesticulations. Lost somewhere were flocks of poorly dressed screaming children running through narrow streets, backyards of the dirty apartment houses, wooden porches, and wide vestibules. No merchandise could be bought in the late evening, which was obtainable before without trouble from shopkeepers standing in front of their closed stores.

Vanished was the ambience of mystery and the particular charm of the dark, desolated little streets and alleys without the weak light of the lanterns. Disappeared forever were the wooden Succoths, covered with branches of fir trees, which were built in the backyards, on the porches and balconies in memory of the Jews who dwelt in the desert. No Jews could be seen on the second day of the New Year praying at the banks of the Vistula, fortunately memorialized by the heritage of paintings such as the popular *Trabki* (Trumpets) by Gierymski. This is what the occupation authorities wanted.

The regulation about the transfer of all inhabitants and their businesses from the ghetto area by March 20, 1941, did not include major factories and shops producing army supplies, the court building, the neighboring jail, and my pharmacy. I and my personnel, which consisted of three ladies (Mgr. [Magister or Master of Pharmacology, an academic title] Irena Drozdzikowska, Mgr. Helena Krywaniuk, and Mgr. Aurelia Daner-Czortkowa) received passes for the ghetto.

On the date prescribed by the German authorities, the resettlement of the population was completed. My parents and I had to relocate beyond the ghetto walls. No "Aryan" was permitted to live in the ghetto. The only exception was the jail guard at the court (the court and the jail were excluded from the ghetto area after the June resettlements in 1942) and me because I lived in the duty room at the pharmacy. It again escaped the attention of the German authorities, and somewhat later, when the health authorities ordered permanent night duty service in the only pharmacy in the ghetto, it was silently sanctioned. Thus the pharmacy "Under the Eagle" was placed by fate in the very heart of the ghetto where it became witness to the inhuman deportations, monstrous crimes, and the constant degradation of human dignity and self-respect of the occupants.

The ghetto contained approximately 320 apartment buildings; the population, approximately 16,000.

On the twentieth of March 1941, I was alone in the pharmacy. At about 6:00 P.M., the traffic increased rapidly. After a few minutes, there were so many people in the place that I couldn't close the door. I found out soon enough that at the end of the streets leading out of the ghetto, German guards were stationed who let no one pass beyond the ghetto area. Excitement! Hysteria! After a while people calmed down, explaining to themselves that this regulation was somehow connected with the Jewish Passover holiday, which began that very day.

After closing the pharmacy at 8:00 P.M., I left the ghetto wondering whether the Germans would let me back in. The German guard stopped me and looked at my papers, which permitted me to move around freely in the ghetto. I asked whether I would be able to come back. I received a short answer, "Nein" (No). Coming back, however, at about 10:00 P.M., not walking this time, I took the trolley, which crossed the ghetto, making a wide curve when turning into Limanowska Street. At the corner of Lwowska and Limanowska Streets, I jumped off the speeding trolley to the general consternation of the passengers.

So passed the first day in the closed ghetto.

Immediately after the Passover holiday the ghetto began to assume a strange new appearance. Scores of workers, bricklayers, and carpenters were building walls, setting bars in windows of apartments looking out on the "Aryan" quarter, installing posts and constructing gates. People looked with terror on the new walls rising, built in the style of Jewish cemetery monuments.

The walls were completed, as were the bars on the windows. Three gates led to the ghetto. The main one was at Podgorze Square. Above the entrance there was a huge six-pointed Star of David and a large inscription in Hebrew: "Jewish Quarter." On both sides of the gate were dark blue lamps. Through the center gate passed the trolley, the route of which led through the main streets of the ghetto, Limanowska and Lwowska.

Located at the main gate was the central post of the German police and the seat of the *Judenrat* (Jewish Council), created by the Germans in place of the former Jewish Kehilla. Here, during the first few weeks of the ghetto's existence one could gain access with relative ease. The reason for entry most frequently used was the necessity of reclaiming cash from the Jews.

The second gate was placed at the end of Limanowska Street, at its confluence with Lwowska Street. The third gate from Plac Zgody led to the third bridge on the Vistula. At both of these gates, blue-uniformed police were posted.

Most of the people returning from work came through Plac Zgody. Here the papers were examined, the quantities of foodstuffs brought in were checked, and at night, smuggling of various types of merchandise took place.

Days passed, then weeks. At first people regarded the walls around them with fear. The most frequently expressed somber conjectures were: "They probably want us to starve." I see, as if it was today, the frightened face of a lady, a close relation of Dr. Drobner, who came to me often, accompanied by a beautiful dog. Every day she would ask me, "Please tell me what the people in Cracow are saying. What will happen to us?" She suffered a psychic trauma which remained with her till the end of her stay in the ghetto, i.e. to the June deportation and her death in 1942.

Time was doing its job. People got used to the new life in such changed conditions. They looked at their existences from a different point of view. The *Arbeitsamt* (Labor Department) organized the ghetto, and stamped the identity cards which replaced the old passports for the people who worked in the city. These cards permitted holders to exit to their places of work.

With white bands bearing the Star of David on the right sleeve, thousands of people passed through the ghetto gate. So, in the morning hours the ghetto was deserted till the curfew hour, i.e. 9:00 P.M. In the ghetto there remained (not having the authorization to leave) those who did not work in the city—the old, the sick, and the children.

And so, the days passed. Every day new regulations appeared, new commands whose sole purpose was to make life even more difficult for people whose life was not very joyful in any event.

The Judenrat, created by the Germans, was composed of twenty-four members, with the attorney Dr. Arthur Rosenzweig as president. This group served as the official representative body of the Jews. It was located in the main police station.

From its very inception, the Judenrat was under the thumb of the Gestapo. Cases connected with the ghetto were under the jurisdiction of Department III, Room No. 302, Pomorska Street.

In this building, the most cruel crimes against the Jews were conceived. Hearings were conducted with beatings and torture. In the basement of the building, after the war, traces of human blood were found, as well as scratches on the walls made by fingernails and bullet marks where Poles and Jews perished.

Activities of the Judenrat were primarily concerned with carrying out the orders of the Gestapo. These activities included general administration, preparation of the statistical data, lists of residents, registration of stores, distribution of food and fuel for the inhabitants, editing and publishing regulations of the occupying authorities and their execution. In time more and more difficult and distressing tasks were assigned to the members of the Judenrat.

A Jewish police unit, the so-called *Ordnungsdienst* (Service for Keeping Order) or OD, was organized with Symcha Spira as the head. Dressed in a perfectly fitting uniform decorated with all kinds of distinguishing insignia—Spira, a glazier by profession and until the war, full-bearded and wearing a long black capote—suddenly became a "big shot." He was given the task of selecting people to help him form a uniformed Jewish police force whose members were commonly called "Odemans." Among them, the Civil Division could be identified by their blue jackets with lapels and neckties, while the rest wore coats buttoned to the neck. However, both wore on their right sleeves a patch on which "Ordnungsdienst" was stitched in Hebrew letters. The Civil Division was particularly favored by the Gestapo.

The tasks of the OD, apart from carrying out the orders of the Gestapo unquestioningly and ruthlessly, included keeping internal order, detecting any transgressions, and technically implementing all the regulations issued by the Judenrat. In time, the impact of the OD on the ghetto dwellers was intensified.

Within the ghetto boundaries, hospitals, orphanages, and old people's shelters were formed. A Jewish post office was established, located at Limanowska Street, with its own postage stamps in Hebrew.

Included was a small office of the fiscal department, the head of which was Mr. Rajski. A public bath was also founded, equipped with delousing and disinfecting facilities.

Secret teaching of Judaic subjects flourished. They were taught by the great Talmudic scholars Lazar Panzer and Schein Klingberg. A renowned authority on Jewish liturgy and mysticism, Klingberg was shot in Plaszow by a Gestapo member, Strojewski. A number of students took music, drawing, and painting lessons outside of the ghetto as long as it was possible to leave it with a pass. Quite a number of these young people, without cost, studied with the well-known Cracow artist, Prof. Chomicz, residing on Grodzka Street. Prof. Chomicz has maintained contact with some of these people to this day, people that he helped so much, and took to heart.

The Orthodox youth were associated with an organization called "Talmud Torah." Three synagogues existed, and the religious life did not suffer any significant change. Services were held, people generally observed the religious tenets—fasting, celebrating the Shabbes, and observing the holidays. During these holidays, ardent devotion was evident. The lamentations and zeal written on their faces betokened, only too well, the depth and intensity of their worship.

From the windows of the pharmacy facing the large courtyard in the rear of the building, I saw an old man with a gray beard and *peyoth* (side curls) rhythmically rocking to the plaintive sounds of the cantor's hymns. In almost every apartment house the Kaddish (prayer in memory of the dead) was fervently recited. I saw old women in lace-embroidered shawls standing motionless with glassy staring eyes, immersed in the monotone sounds of the prayers while in the depths of grief and anxiety for themselves and their loved ones.

Often, and particularly in the periods of the Jewish holidays, I would listen to conversations and discussions on religious topics. The atmosphere—serious, mystical, heightened also by the semi-darkness of the pharmacy—overwhelmed one with its irresistible power. I would recall and associate it with *Dziady* (forefathers), a drama by Adam Mickiewicz, the foremost Polish poet, written in 1820–1835. In this work, the Messianic motif appears frequently.

Some years after the war, I was visited by Rev. Karol Wojtyla, the present Pope John Paul II. Knowing that I spent time in the ghetto during its entire existence, he put the following question to me: "Do you know how the Jews regarded the Messianic idea in this time of horror, beastliness, all the murders and negation of human dignity?" This question could be addressed to me indirectly. The answer would have to come only from one of the outstanding Talmudic scholars. I decided to get in touch with one who was knowledgeable in these matters and fortunately I found such a man.

In appearance he looked as if he might have materialized and descended from a Gottlieb portrait: distinguished looking, with an elongated gray head; black, deep penetrating eyes; patriarchal beard and with meditation and sadness reflected in his expression.

After hearing my question, he remained silent for a long time, and afterward he directed his strangely charming gaze at me. With a trace of a smile at the corners of his mouth, he addressed me with solemnity: "The question of arrival of the Messiah . . . well." Here he stopped for a while and then continued, "How should I clarify this? You would not understand it anyway if I would speak as necessary . . . Please imagine that a Friday is followed by a Friday. Improbable, isn't it? But, not impossible. I shall tell you this in still another way. If such a time should come in which all the Jews in the whole world, every single one, meaning children, young, old men and women, would not sin—not by thought, nor by speech, nor by deed—then this could be the time, you understand, the time in which the Messiah might appear. He could come, he will come one day . . . But, you would not be able to grasp that. . . ." He turned his gaze far away stroking his long, well-cared-for beard. And with a voice growing softer as if he were talking to himself: "Friday after Friday, and still it could happen. We are waiting for this day, we are waiting." Then getting animated again: "No, Panie (Mr.)

Pankiewicz, this is not an easy answer, this is not simple, but it is so good that you came. I am happy that you paid me this visit. Take care."

The deep content of his statement, the whole mood created by this meeting and his very presence, made an unforgettable impression on me.

This rabbi lived on Dietlowska Street. This meeting took place at the temple on Miodowa Street. I took the liberty of transmitting his statements to the future cardinal and present Holy Father.

Several times in each month during the initial phases of the ghetto, always on a Saturday, I was visited by my friend, a judge who was well known in Cracow for his court cases and for his charm. In these meetings, a very beautiful lady participated, a renowned fashionable dresser with blond hair and a melancholy look, Miss Maryla Schenker. In my quiet room with the lights switched off, drapes pulled shut and candles lit, we would feast on fish prepared in the "Jewish way" and procured from a nearby restaurant. After several shots of Slivovitz (a dry plum brandy) and a glassful of white wine, it soon seemed that the world was laughing and that we were in heaven. This mood lasted until the moment of parting.

The reality of the outside world abruptly destroyed all traces of the pleasant moments we enjoyed. The judge with pass in hand would leave the ghetto; Maryla would walk quickly towards her home.

When the Jewish ghetto was anxiety-ridden, when arrests were occurring, and when there was talk about approaching resettlement, Maryla would not return to the ghetto after work (in Cracow), but would stop at the judge's place and wait for news. At a fixed time, I would drop in at my friend's apartment to inform them about the actual situation. A short time later, the judge was arrested by the Gestapo and transported to Oswiecim (Auschwitz), where he suffered through very bad times. Beaten, with a broken arm and ruined physically, he miraculously survived the war. Miss Schenker would come into the pharmacy to obtain information about the arrested man. News from Oswiecim was difficult to come by, and was invariably incorrect.

I also remember such an unusual evening when my dear friend Kocwa, professor at Jagiellonic University, who, after returning from the camp in Dachau, expressed a wish to visit the ghetto. I obtained a pass for him, and after some walking through the streets of the enclosed quarter I led him to the pharmacy. We entered the duty room, where the drapes were drawn and the Shabbes candles lit. We found ourselves in the company of my coworkers and the fabulous musicians Rosner, violinist, with his brother, a fantastic accordionist. At a table set with delicacies from a

Jewish kitchen, immersed in the enchanting melodies of Viennese waltzes, we completely forgot the passage of time, the curfew, the war, the walled-in little town and the fate of its inhabitants sentenced to so much humiliation and tragedy. The dinner extended into the wee hours of the morning. It was an unforgettable night, one which we recalled many years after the end of the war.

Time seemed to move the hands of the clock faster and faster. People who, not so long ago, could not conceive how one could live under such conditions were getting used to them, giving up the most primitive demands of civilization and beginning slowly to forget even the recent past. The daily worries—about a piece of bread, fighting to keep one's job in the city, producing practically no income but providing a possibility of leaving the ghetto—occupied the lion's share of one's free time. The Arbeitsamt, under the direction of a Viennese named Schepessy, kept office hours from morning until late night. German, Polish, and Jewish clerks were busy preparing files on the workers, made job assignments, supplying contingents of people for work outside of the ghetto at each demand of the German authorities.

Three times a week, a "Jewish Newspaper" was delivered to the ghetto. This was the only paper for Jews in the Polish language, reporting the war communiques, and announcing all the new successes of the invincible German armies: "Germany is victorious on all fronts."

On the wall of the OD building, which formerly housed a Catholic orphanage and later one of the Jewish Association "CENTOS," was a slogan, "DEUTSCHLAND SIEGT AN ALLEN FRONTEN." How astonished was the SS Sturmscharführer Willy Kunde, the Gestapo protector of the OD, when he noticed one day that the "S" in "SIEGT" (is victorious) was changed to "L." "DEUTSCHLAND LIEGT (is lying) AN ALLEN FRONTEN." The Germans pretended not to see this, but the sign quickly disappeared.

Various advertisements began to appear on the walls of the city and also in the underground conspiratorial newspaper, which featured the same headline as the government publication, "Goniec Krakowski"; thus, combining malice with the macabre tended to ridicule and humiliate the occupier. We read advertisements such as:

> "Will sell Jewish jewelry, cleaned of blood." Goeth, Commandant of the Jewish Camp in Wola Duchacka.

> "Infants in the ghetto, I kill with one shot and when drunk, I discover a conspirator in each Pole." Joachim Thun, Building Inspector, Prokocim Barracks.

"We sell clothing pilfered by German gangsters." Army Supply Authority, Cracow.

One of the first regulations in the ghetto was ordering the immediate removal of all inscriptions in the Polish language and replacing them with those in Hebrew. The only exception was the pharmacy. The appearance of the ghetto was completely changed. After all, even in the ghetto there were many people who were not familiar with the Hebrew alphabet. As a result, they suddenly found themselves almost like in a strange, unfamiliar country where each inscription, billboard, and every little sign was incomprehensible. The physicians were most troubled by this. The frequent changes of apartments reflected very badly on their practice.

Economic life in the ghetto started to develop. New stores were opening, new restaurants, patisseries, dairies, cafeterias . . . well, even a restaurant-bar featuring guest performances by local artists and an orchestra conducted by the aforementioned violinist Rosner, together with his brother.

Life under these new conditions, so far removed from the normal, flowed unbelievably swiftly. Constant tension and serious concerns about earning a living were affecting and depressing everyone.

Here and there, the SS men would indulge their wild instincts and attack the passersby, beating and kicking them. The old people, particularly those with beards and peyoth, suffered the worst humiliations. The SS tormentors pulled them into gates, where they would shear their beards, cut their peyoth and tear their hair. This "amusement" would always be accompanied by beating, kicking, and the terrifying howls of the tormentors. It was happening more often, so the Judenrat issued a regulation forbidding the wearing of beards and peyoth. The more orthodox would not comply so they circumvented the prohibition by covering their beards with scarves so that only the eyes and nose were visible. Next day after this order was proclaimed, an epidemic of toothaches became prevalent in the ghetto. Scores of people could be seen with their faces wrapped up. Faithfulness to tradition proved to be stronger than regulations and threats. At first such events became the dreaded sensation of the day; the indignation of the inhabitants seemed limitless, but already the pessimists started to predict a foreboding future.

More and more, Jews were beaten at work; often bands of SS men lay in wait at the bridge to torment the unsuspecting people returning to the ghetto. Once I witnessed the following scene, which occurred in front of the windows of my pharmacy.

It was about ten o'clock in the morning. A car passing rapidly by stopped in front of the pharmacy. In the car were two civilians. I came closer to the door and I recognized one of them. This was Gustaw Beckman, well-known Gestapo man from Podgorze. Before the war, he was known in Cracow as the proprietor of the Toledo Razor Blade Factory. This was a magnificent specimen of a Nazi—squat, fat, with a big belly, a neck like a bull, and a misshapen head. This pawnbroker type, a repulsive individual, became the terror of Podgorze. He was sentenced to a year in prison for offenses in Poland before the war and later took bloody revenge on the District Attorney, Andrzej Bienkowski, and Judges Wladyslaw Bobilewicz and Konrad Frackiewicz, who tried his case. Beckman called through the car window to a Jew passing by. The Jew approached and seeing a stout German with a swastika on his lapel, took off his hat. Instantly, the German hit him in the face full force with his fist and drove off smiling.

This was the terror of life in the initial months of the ghetto's existence. People became accustomed to it to some degree, considering each wild episode to be something quite natural and understandable.

Time passed toward an unknown future, which was assessed every day in a more melancholy way. The daily life experiences seemed to prove it. Yet there was no lack of optimists in the ghetto who believed that, even under these circumstances, one would somehow survive. They mistakenly believed, throughout the ghetto's existence, that the war would end soon, that Germany's defeat was inevitable and that any day America, England, France, and Turkey would definitely declare themselves, and then there would be an invasion and with it—liberation.

The pharmacy was, in the opinion of most of the people, a sort of embassy, a diplomatic station, representing the world, singularly free, within the walled and imprisoned city.

It became a daily meeting place for many very interesting people. Here, one could find assembled at certain hours of the day, people of all ages and in all walks of life. Here, from early morning the German newspapers and underground press were read, the latest war communiques could be studied and commented upon, and the political situation assessed. Here, also, the daily problems and worries were discussed. Conversations continuing far into the night weighed the future prognostications. "Let something happen, finally," they were saying. It seemed that this inhuman time had halted, that the clock of history stopped at the fatal hour . . . perdition!

Apart from the pharmacy "Under the Eagle," there was another workplace in the ghetto periphery that employed Poles. This was a factory producing optical glass, and it was located in my immediate vicinity on Targowa Street No. 6. The head of this institution was a well-known activist of the PPS (Polish Socialist Party), Mr. Feliks Dziuba, who was at the same time, the manager of another company, Spektrum, which produced glass for clocks and car windows. Its main factory was located far beyond the ghetto area. Both of these companies also worked for the army. Because of that, Feliks Dziuba could obtain, with relative ease, passes for himself and for the employees of his glass factory. Together with his coworkers Wanda Klosowa, Jozef Mika, and Tomasz Perski, they bravely joined the ranks of those who helped the Jews.

Thanks to Feliks Dziuba, many Jews were assigned by the current administrator of the Arbeisamt, Schepessy, to work at the Spektrum company. They were listed as specialists, although they knew nothing about this trade. Dziuba did not actually employ them, but permitted them to spend the time quietly until the hour arrived for the return of the workers to the ghetto. After a short time, this practice of issuing the passes came to the attention of the Gestapo through an informer, Marcel Gruner. Schepessy was arrested and was shot some weeks later. One of the great achievements of Dziuba and his coworker Jozef Zajac was their help in securing the release from the ghetto of Benjamin Halbreich, who was a member of the ZOB (Jewish Fighting Organization), and then employing him at the Spektrum. The work day in the optical glass factory lasted from early morning till evening. During the *Aktions* later carried out by the Germans in the ghetto, the factory did not function and it was closed toward the end of the ghetto's existence, when the Gestapo took over exclusively. After the liquidation of the ghetto, the company resumed operations. Feliks Dziuba also gained fame as one of the very few who saved the fragments of the Grunwald Monument on Matejka Square when it was blown up.

The year 1941 was coming to a close. On December 27, automobiles with loudspeakers mounted on the roofs entered the ghetto and announced that, in accordance with the directive of the city commandant, all Jews were to turn in all their furs and fur trimmings, without exception, at the building of the Judenrat at Limanowska Street No. 2. Simultaneously, announcements of this directive were posted on the walls within the ghetto, threatening resisters with severe punishment or death.

The death penalty later became the sole punishment for noncompliance with the regulations of the occupying authorities. From morning till dusk, people stood in frost and snow, waiting for hours to comply with the order. Some, not willing to give the furs to the Germans, were destroying them at home, cutting them into pieces, burning them or burying them in the basement. Others, not willing to wait in the seemingly endless line, afraid to destroy these possessions and fearing discovery, dropped them on the ground and covered them with snow. There were also cases of furs being thrown into open basements. Owners of these cellars later paid heavily for this. During searches, police held the owners of the buildings responsible for anything that was hidden there. Smuggling and selling furs for pennies flourished at this time.

The twenty-eighth of December was a Sunday. Early in the morning, German police entered the ghetto and performed a very detailed search. Houses, apartments, attics, and basements were aggressively inspected; they looked into the ovens to make sure that no furs were being burned there. They also included my pharmacy in their intensive search. The Germans just could not believe that I didn't own a fur coat. I was sure that if I did own one they would have taken it from me. People sewed blankets to replace the fur linings in their coats. Women embroidered designs on their collars creating the illusion of Crimean sheepskin. This Aktion, despite the fact that it represented considerable material losses for some people, inspired many jokes at the expense of the Germans. Cartoons appeared showing German soldiers on the Russian front wrapped in ladies' furs and wearing Jewish fur hats, trembling from the cold.

New Year's Eve of 1942 arrived with many good wishes and handshakes exchanged, and the atmosphere in the pharmacy was pleasant and warm. Towards evening, many guests arrived. People were beginning to forget their daily worries and problems. The pharmacy, of course, contained alcohol. We drank it in modest quantities—some maintained that it helped to make the time pass faster.

Many came to me who were exceptionally wise and interesting; the topics of conversation were varied: music, literature, prewar politics, and prognostications. The underground press, which was supplied by my coworkers, was read with great interest. Here, however, it was treated with mistrust, a different reception than it received outside of the ghetto.

A constant visitor to the pharmacy was Filip Schor, who was once a credit manager for a bank in Vienna, a man who knew the arias from almost all of the operas and operettas; in spite of the fact that he did not have a voice, his musicality was phenomenal, his attuned ear was astonishing.

There was not a melody which, once started, he could not finish, name the composer, and the year of its creation and genesis. Erudite, gifted with an encyclopedic memory, with multifaceted interests, known for his humor and sharp wit, he would spend many nights with me while the ODs were seizing people. He would return to the pharmacy, provided that the warnings of impending seizures would reach the inhabitants early enough. Frequently, through a door which opened to the pharmacy corridor, we peered, watching how the ODs were leading those arrested from the apartments in accordance with the prepared lists.

Often a German police patrol, composed mostly of Viennese, would come into the pharmacy, attracted by the light escaping through the window blinds. They would participate in conversations and they would be treated to vodka so that they would not be too interested in the people whose presence in the pharmacy at that late hour could not be logically and convincingly explained.

The conversations that revolved around Austria, memories of old Vienna and of the Kaiser and melodies of Strauss waltzes were the beginning and end of almost every discussion. I have to admit that the visiting policemen (Viennese) behaved quite correctly to the Jews they met there; they always addressed them as "Mr." and spoke with them as if they never heard of discrimination.

Mr. M. Izraeler, a businessman, a diamond expert, a diamond cutter by trade, who spent many years abroad working at this craft, was our inseparable companion. We became acquainted in a rather unique way. In the first weeks of the ghetto's existence, he came to the pharmacy for medicine almost every day. While waiting for the prescription to be filled, he was talking to one of my ladies, Mgr. Irene Drozdikowski. One day he announced at the very outset that he had a big request to make of Miss Irene. He asked her if she would be willing to accept a golden medallion with a picture of the Virgin Mary. From that day forward, we were bound by strong ties of friendship and so it remained till the very end. He was a man of sterling character, an exemplary husband and father. He would appear every day at about ten o'clock in the morning, take a fresh copy of the *Krakauer Zeitung*, which was mounted on a reading frame for the convenience of the readers, and remain silent for about an hour totally absorbed in the newspaper. This was followed by commentaries, discussions, and forecasts of the end of the war. Izraeler was unbelievably optimistic. With his wife, slim, gracious Mrs. Ann, always impeccably dressed, auburn hair, and with her charming young daughter Dorina, with blond hair and big blue eyes, they were a fine example of an ideal and loving family.

Izraeler and his sister, Mrs. Gutman, a woman of unusual beauty, worked in the old age home at great sacrifice, doing whatever they could to ease human suffering. Mrs. Gutman also took care of the children in the orphanage which was located at Jozefinska Street No. 12. She was an eyewitness to the shootings of her innocent defenseless charges. Fate did not allow Izraeler to live to the end of the war. He perished by a German bullet. Mrs. Ann and her daughter Dorina, now always dressed in black, and Mrs. Gutman as well, survived the occupation and immigrated to the United States. Mrs. Gutman's daughter, Anna Sislow, waited for her in New York. Mrs. Ann Izraeler and her daughter lived through very hard times abroad. The noble figures of the Izraeler family etched themselves forever in our memory.

A very dear and frequent guest was Gizela Fendler, a striking brunette with dark complexion, always fashionably dressed. Before the war she was one of the elite of Cracow society and was one of the first ladies to own a magnificent luxurious car and a gallery of costly paintings. She had the unusual gift of overcoming the most difficult and seemingly hopeless situations, almost bordering on bravado. The following episode exhibits her unique courage and self-control.

When she was suddenly forced to leave her apartment in Cracow where she was born and lived through the best years of her childhood and youth, she left an armored safe in one of the many rooms. It contained a hidden compartment that could be detected only by someone familiar with the secret. In this secret compartment were concealed the very expensive jewelry of Mrs. Giza and large quantities of dental gold because her husband was a well-known and popular dentist in Cracow. When the Germans took over the apartment, they left a housekeeper who had been living there for many years. One rainy autumn evening, Mrs. Giza knocked on the door of her old apartment. The door was opened by a speechless and almost overcome Helcia Kohan who was the old nanny.

"For God's sake, what are you doing here, Ma'am? Run away from here immediately. The Germans are drunk and all over the apartment. If they find you here, they will kill you."

"Not a word more!" said Mrs. Giza, putting her finger to her lips. "Go quietly and see what they are doing now, and find out what condition they are in."

Hela had scarcely moved when Giza stealthily crept into the dark room in which the safe was hidden. She opened it, removed the contents from the secret compartment and slowly went downstairs, dissolving into the darkness of the staircase. Only a few seconds passed when the door from her apartment opened and one of the Germans quickly ran downstairs, passing her on the way.

Worthy of admiration were other achievements of Mrs. Gizela. A few weeks after the Germans entered Cracow, she appeared at the headquarters of the city commandant, seeking permission to remove property from her safe-deposit box in the PKO (bank). One of the first regulations of the German authorities concerned the blocking of all bank accounts and safe-deposit boxes. Mrs. Fendler, speaking fluent German, had so charmed and convinced the city commandant that he was taken in, most probably assuming that Mrs. Gizela was of German descent, had lived in Poland for years, and was a local citizen. Not only did he give her permission, but also, at her request, he assigned one of his clerks to accompany her for this transaction. To the great astonishment of the new PKO authorities, after showing the documents supported by the explanations of the clerk who accompanied her, she opened the safe readily, took out the contents, returned the key to the management of PKO and walked out to the street. Mrs. Fendler and her dear son Adam survived the ghetto and the occupation and left Poland to settle permanently in the United States.

An older professional colleague of mine, Mr. Herman, Mgr., grayish, with a benevolent smile, visited me several times a day. Before the war, he was a pharmaceutical inspector in Lwow. In the ghetto he was managing the sanitary department, and because of that position, he constantly cruised the streets with an inseparable cigarette stuck to his lip. Whenever his duties took him near the pharmacy, he dropped in and always had something interesting to tell in the political area, or he would bring some news about the ghetto. During one of the resettlement actions he disappeared and no one ever heard from him again.

A well-known Cracow lawyer, Natan Oberlender, also took part in the daily political discussions in the pharmacy. He was a sober realist. He did not believe the war would end in less than six years. He used to say: "This war has to last at least as long as the last one, if not longer. That's why I figure it at six years." This engendered a storm of protest from E. Wachs, who was the owner of a lamp factory in Podgorze. He read the newspaper "between the lines" and interpreted each sentence to mean that the German defeat was inevitable. "This is written here very clearly, you only have to know how to read." His sole fervent wish was to see his sons who, in September 1939, fled the occupation to the east. "This desire," he would say, "is so strong that a person is capable of withstanding the worst." He did not live to have his wish fulfilled. He was taken away on October 28, 1942, and he perished as did all in this resettlement.

Dr. Roman Glassner, a medical doctor, well-known in Cracow, also visited with us every day. He was slightly stooped, gray hair as a pigeon, and always smiling, a man of great culture and universal knowledge, a devotee of and expert in classical music. He dropped in for a glass of chartreuse and for "fables," as he used to say. His innate cheerfulness and joy for life, which never left him, even in the ghetto, was snuffed out by the news of the arrest of his daughter, whom he loved as dearly as life. She was a physician, Stanislawa Glasser-Skiminow, who was the wife of a physician, son of a professor at the UJC (Jagellonic University) in Cracow. A vicious denunciation resulted in her arrest and separation from her husband. At first she was transported to the prison on Montelupich for a hearing and later to the ghetto where she was placed in a separate cell at the hospital on Jozefinska Street. Here also were confined seriously retarded human creatures with hair covering half of their foreheads, who had been transferred from the asylum, located before the war at Kopernik Street. The cell in which Mrs. Skiminow was held was guarded day and night by a Jewish policeman OD. Dr. Glassner moved the proverbial heaven and earth, spending the remnants of their fortune to rescue his daughter. And a miracle happened, because one could not call it anything else. In an amazing manner, Mrs. Stasia ran from the prison under cover of night. The successful escape and the manner of its execution was credited to two Polish ladies, Zofia Krzyzanski and Olga Keplicz, whose acquaintance with Förster, a man about whom there will be mention later on, was utilized to rescue Poles and Jews in the ghetto.

Marcel Gruner was an infamous figure in the ghetto. He was a commercial agent about thirty-two years old, tall, handsome, and well-built. He started to come to the pharmacy, offering various cosmetic wares. By nature, he was very cowardly, and he aroused suspicions in me. At first I couldn't figure out what to make of him. His questions were constantly directed towards finding out how much someone earned, how big his turnover, and what was his lifestyle. He came to the pharmacy every day, always late at night, often bringing us dainty tidbits. It was generally supposed that I exerted a great influence over him. I could always do with him as I wished. Once when there was a problem concerning an apartment for a certain Mrs. Kempler, who did not have a roof over her head, I was able to convince him to take her, together with her child, into his place (he had two bedrooms). After a time, he threw her out, supposedly because of the child's sickness. I gave him a piece of my mind, telling him that as long as he would not take them back, I didn't want to know him. He came in, made excuses, but he took them back.

There was talk that Marcel Gruner worked for the Germans. He seemed assured and confident in various situations. When I met him in the city without an armband, which was obligatory for all Jews, and I pretended that I didn't notice. I decided to find out what role he played with the German authorities. One evening, when he came into the pharmacy, we decided to get him drunk and to search him. Gruner, in spite of his stature and good health, had an uncommonly weak head. He got drunk as a goat and fell asleep. In his wallet we found a German confidential permit which entitled him to move about the streets of Cracow without an armband. After a few hours, Gruner awakened, remembering nothing, said good-bye to me and left the pharmacy.

As it became apparent later, he was at first in the customs and income tax services, and was later arrested by the Gestapo. He was released after three days and evidently became a spy remaining officially in the services of the Gestapo. He was a man who was not particularly bad, but infinitely stupid and with no willpower. Taken into the Gestapo service, he betrayed scores of Jews. He was conscious of the fact that we knew about his role, but he was astute enough to avoid acquaintances whom he met in the pharmacy. He therefore limited his visits to a minimum. When he finally did come, he assured me that I would soon hear from him from abroad, that he would write to me, and that I would then understand everything and wouldn't condemn him. I wished, for his sake, that this would happen very soon. He did not go abroad. He continued his deplorable activities until the well-deserved punishment caught up with him. He was shot, together with his wife, it was said, by the underground organization sometime after March 1943. When we first became acquainted, he was a perfect complement to the above-mentioned Schor. Endowed with a good voice, unusually musical, they would give concerts for two voices, singing melodies of the most famous operas and operettas.

Among the constant visitors was a physician, Dr. Leon Steinberg, with whom we were bound inextricably in true friendship. The group of our charming guests was further enhanced by Dr. Wladyslaw Sztencel, pessimistic, an enchanting Freudian with the countenance of an old Polish nobleman; bushy mustache, a jovial face, darting eyes, and elegant mannerisms; and there was also Dr. W. Armer.

"Freud" was always smiling and seemed content, as did his wife "Mrs. Dr. Freud." He knew everything; he also knew the world in which he traveled while working in the Polish consulate in Berlin.

Dr. Armer, a man of impeccable character, an expert in the studies of the

Talmud and Kabbala, brought to me twelve priceless Torah scrolls from the ghetto and asked me to hold them for safekeeping. We learned, with great sorrow, that he was shot in the camp at Plaszow, which I will discuss later in greater detail. He recommended two Poles to me who had passes for the ghetto because of their employment. These two gentlemen, Wladyslaw Szalek and Roman Zbroja, reported to me several times a month, and came to the pharmacy even more often. They brought large envelopes containing forged papers, *Kennkarten* (identification cards), flawlessly counterfeited stamps on various documents, and newspapers published by underground organizations. The envelopes were picked up by the addressees most frequently in the evening or at night. The newspapers, after being read by our regular guests, were forwarded. There was a secret printing press in the apartment of Mrs. W. Szalka, where, besides the above two, several more people worked. Among them was the well-known engraver Henryk Teichler, who was living in the ghetto, and who, anticipating resettlement, would disappear to seek shelter at Mrs. Szalka's until the action ended.

Both gentlemen, W. Szalek and R. Zbroja, ceased their activities in the ghetto when it came under the supervision of the Gestapo. As of October 15, 1942, all passes lost their validity.

Occasionally, I was visited by a doctor of law and philosophy, Rappaport, a writer and journalist, and a well-known personality in Lwow. Gray-haired, tall, a gentleman approximately 68 years old, he lived in the ghetto with his elderly sister. He was a man of unusual intelligence who spoke gently and interestingly. I listened eagerly when he spoke about his scientific work, travels, observations, and opinions of the world. It was intriguing that he seemed completely unconcerned about the war, the communiques from the front, or any of the problems connected with earning a living. He lived as if he were on another planet, immersed in scientific work. Obsessed with mathematics, he continually pored over complicated problems.

"I was never bored in all my life," he used to tell me. "Even if I should live for a thousand years, I would have so many interests that I would lack time for these mundane problems which engulf me."

Once he came to me and confessed that he would like to send a registered letter to Geneva or to the Swiss embassy in Berlin because, as he maintained, he had solved a mathematical problem which was considered unsolvable by Pythagoras. He had trisected an angle by means of a straight edge (not calibrated) and a compass. He ascertained that he had performed all the possible calculations, and he was sure that he was not mistaken. I could not send the letter to the Swiss embassy but I did not tell this to Rappaport, in order not to worry him. Every day he would ask if there was a reply. He believed that publication of this work would make him rich, and that certainly the Germans would free him and his sister from the ghetto so that he could live as a free man. I told him that I knew a professor from the Cracow University who was a mathematician, that I would go to him, arrange to get a pass for him to enter the ghetto so that the two of them could meet here in my pharmacy to discuss this matter. Rappaport became excited about this idea and the meeting actually took place. My friend, Tadeusz Wazewski, a well-known professor at the Jagellonic University, right at the start explained to me that this problem was certainly as unsolvable as perpetual motion. But he would gladly visit the ghetto and talk with Dr. Rappaport. Two meetings took place.

After a detailed review of Dr. Rappaport's work, Prof. Wazewski declared that although this problem could not be completely resolved, the method proposed by Dr. Rappaport was one of the best and most exact of all methods up to now—and it would be published in a professional journal. This happened after the war. Rappaport was not destined to live to enjoy the success. He perished during the June deportation.

We had very interesting chats with the painter Abraham Neuman, who was known not only in Poland but abroad as well. He traveled around the world, but he spent most of his time in Paris where he arranged several exhibitions, gaining considerable renown. Unquestionably, his was a major artistic talent of unusual individuality. In spite of his advanced years, he was gifted with a temperament for excitement and a fervent zest for life.

He lived very modestly in the ghetto, but he obstinately believed that conditions would improve and that he would travel throughout the world again. He painted relatively little in the ghetto; to earn a living, he painted portraits from photographs, and received good prices for them. He assumed that if any fool wanted such a well-known artist as he to enlarge a photograph, then let the ignoramus pay—he used to say—"Pay well!" "I could make your wife thirty years younger," he would say, "if you want to, and for the same money, and you don't even have to bring the photograph."

Feliks Schor, who was present at the time, interrupted him, "Excuse me, sir, for interrupting, but apropos of what you said, I should like to tell you a little story."

Neuman stopped talking, looking at Schor askance, and said, "Speak now, but quickly, because most certainly you are not going to say anything very smart."

Schor replied, "You know, sir, there was once an artist like you who painted very fashionably. He was about to paint the portrait of a husband for a farmer's wife who was widowed for only three days and did not have her husband's photograph. The painter had never seen the man. She would therefore have to describe him. The "Babina" started to describe the deceased as best she could. She knew how he looked, what kind of eyes he had, nose, mouth, forehead and so on. The painter, using a sheet of white paper, wrote down what the mourning widow was saying. "Come to pick up the portrait in ten days," said the painter. Ten days passed and the "Babina" knocked on the artist's door. He sat her in front of the easel, on which was a painting covered with a black cloth. "Attention," said the painter, looking hypnotically into the woman's eyes; "Attention!" he said louder, approaching the picture. "Babina" became so rigid she did not stir. "One, two, three . . ." and the painter tore the cloth from the picture . . . The woman shivered, looked and looked, opened her eyes wide—opened her mouth—and then grabbing her head, screamed, "Oh my God! He is only gone two weeks and look how he's changed—poor man!—beyond recognition—who would expect it, who?"

Schor stopped and patted Neuman on the shoulder. Neuman gave Schor a dirty look and made him an unprintable proposition, then sat down and sipped his warm tea. He spoke no more, in spite of our pleading.

"Some other time, when this moron is not around."

Schor could not hide his elation—he had a great sense of humor, was never insulting, would emerge victorious from the toughest verbal encounter, and always ended his arguments with a joke.

Neuman played a palm reader here. He would tell fortunes from palms, from facial features—he would guess the past and foretell the future—and one had to admit he did it very successfully. He possessed a great talent for narration; he spoke glibly and interestingly. He complained about the miserable wrangling with the woman with whom he shared the apartment, all because he forced her to pose for him in the nude. She was a simple woman, about 60—no wonder those sessions ended noisily.

I remember a very pleasant evening I spent in the pharmacy in the company of Neuman who came with Mr. Gebirtig, a well-known popular Yiddish poet. Gebirtig recited his enchanting poem, *Es Brent* (The World is Burning). Two years later, it became the battle song of the fighting Warsaw ghetto. The Jewish rebels fought and perished singing this song.

Even today I still hear the melodic murmur of the poet's words, "Zun, zun, zong," full of lyricism and musing. "I wrote this poem with tears," said the poet to me. "Because in writing it, I cried like a baby." He was shot by the Germans during the October resettlement in 1942.

Among the regular visitors to the pharmacy who must be mentioned was Dr. Abraham Mirowski, well-known Cracow ophthalmologist, outstanding specialist, and excellent surgeon. Always cheerful, calm, and tactful, although sadness and brooding never left him, he appeared in the ghetto in February 1942. After arriving, he learned about the death of his wife. After her loss, the fine people, Mr. and Mrs. Ameneisen, particularly Mrs. Ameneisen-Detler, took care of his little son. Sometime later, Dr. Mirowski's young one was taken by the Germans, and all traces of him disappeared. In spite of the incessant search by the father, it was impossible to determine the boy's fate, although the wonderful Dr. Mirowski always believed that he was alive, and waited for his return.

Dr. Mirowski remarried in the ghetto and the wedding ceremony was performed by an accidentally identified rabbi, who kept his calling secret. The wedding took place on May 5, 1943. People enclosed in the ghetto did not like to be lonely, did not want to go for the resettlement alone, and did not want to die in loneliness. After the war, the Mirowski couple settled permanently in Haifa, Israel. In 1957, I visited them during my stay of several months in that country.

Among the most mysterious figures of the ghetto, because such figures also existed there, was Alexander Förster, mentioned above on the occasion of the flight of Mr. Skiminav. Förster was purported to be the son of a piano manufacturer in Leipzig. He was a German Jew, spoke very little Polish, and was chronically hoarse. He was forty years old, of medium height, balding brunette, and dressed stylishly. When he walked he wobbled slightly from his hips, and wore a large signet ring but did not wear an armband. He spoke many languages, traveled extensively and just before the war was a dance impresario. In August 1939, he was in Cracow with an English dancer who performed at the Feniks (well-known Cracow café) and I met him that year. Immediately after the ghetto was established, it was rumored that Förster was a German. That was why he enjoyed such important privileges, as walking in or out of the ghetto without an armband, and alone occupying a three-room apartment immediately adjacent to the ghetto gate. He operated a restaurant-dance-bar in the same building, which he later closed.

He enjoyed the privilege of entering or leaving the ghetto at all hours of the day or night, regardless of the curfew. He had a second apartment in Cracow in the Hotel Royal-City. He was permitted to greet the Gestapo men by raising his hand, and they, in turn, shook his. He was so familiar with many of them that he was allowed to use the more personal form of address, "thou," and he arranged parties at his place for all the Gestapo dignitaries. These parties would often last very late and often until morning. The departing guests would remind the residents of their existence by shooting their revolvers. There were also rumors that Förster had an office in the main Gestapo building at Pomorska Street, and that he would sit there in a German uniform. (How much truth there was to this story was not known.) There was conjecture that he wrote the so-called "Stimmungs-Berichte" or reports about the moods of the population. He became more widely known during the resettlements and the issuance of the ghetto residence permits. Many tried to get close to him, hoping to gain some benefit through his influence. And indeed his powers were extensive. At the time when the residence permits were being issued, he was able to obtain them for many who were unable to get them in any other way. During the June Aktion, I saw Förster moving freely among all ranks of the Gestapo. At the Plac Zgody, he intervened in behalf of Jews and pulled them from the transport, quite often without recompense.

One day, the ghetto was shocked by the news that Förster was arrested by the Gestapo, and was incarcerated in the OD prison. On the next morning, the Gestapo came to the ghetto, and one of them, Hermann Heinrich, entered the OD and ordered Förster's cell opened. After a time, they both walked out laughing and joking. A subsequent commandmant of the *Schupo* (police) in Podgorze, named Bousko, about whom there will be more later, related to me how this arrest came about. Hermann Heinrich was celebrating his promotion in the building of the Gestapo on Pomorska Street. Among many of the gifts he received was a large basket of red roses with the compliments and congratulations of Förster. As a practical joke, he called the OD and ordered Förster's arrest. It was rumored that he wanted to make Förster understand in this fashion that, after all, there was a vast difference between them—he represented the *Herrenvolk* (master race) and Förster, of Jewish descent, was therefore *Untermensch* (subhuman).

Two occurrences in the ghetto, the arrest of Förster and the slap in the face to the OD commander, Spira, by the SS man, Horst Pilarzik, showed forcefully to all that the Germans had no respect for anybody, even for the loyal people who served them slavishly.

In my opinion, there was no fault to be found with Förster as far as the ghetto was concerned. Interceding for money or gifts, and even without compensation as it sometimes happened, he gained for people the right to stay in the ghetto and occasionally facilitated their escape.

After the liquidation of the ghetto on March 13, 1943, Förster lived in Cracow. He had a mission in Hungary and returned three weeks later. He was suspected of collaborating with British intelligence. He left again, but after his return this time, he was arrested and imprisoned at Montelupich. All trace of him vanished. We knew that he was liquidated. Soon after the Gestapo started to spread rumors that the charges against him were groundless and that Förster was released. He was then said to have been parachuted into the British Isles as a spy in the German service. This was another of the many German lies!

Sometime later, I received a letter from the United States from the brothers Rosner, whom I mentioned before. They wrote that they spoke with someone who was imprisoned in Montelupich with Förster, and witnessed him being clubbed to death by the Gestapo.

Early on after the ghetto was established, Mrs. Dora Schmerzler appeared at the pharmacy. She was a very interesting person—a German Jew, a refugee from Germany during the period that Hitler came to power. In Cracow she worked at the stationery company of Alexanderowicz at Dluga Street No. 1. She was a beautiful woman, dressed fashionably, graceful, with a creamy complexion, sapphire eyes and reddish hair, an ideal model for Rachel of Wyspianski's *Wesele* (Wedding). During the resettlements she would leave the ghetto and would return when it was all over. During the June deportation, she left again and, bidding us good-bye, said that in a few days she would drop in at the pharmacy. Because she was absent from the ghetto, she was unable to obtain the *Blauschein* (blue card), which entitled the bearer to remain within the ghetto walls. She therefore left Cracow and moved to Zabierzow, where she lived among a small group of Jews.

The wonderful Dr. Biezynski helped those in hiding. The spiritual supporter of Mrs. Dora was my junior colleague, Artur Biberstein, a man full of goodness. He performed miracles for Mrs. Dora by obtaining a stamp on a certain document for her and a blue card, which allowed her to live in the ghetto. After a while he obtained all the necessary documents for her. Mrs. Dora returned. We heard that on the day after her departure from Zabierzow, the Gestapo arrested all the Jews who were in hiding with her and shot them. Among the others who perished at that time were Ing. (Engineer) Ignacy Ganger and Bober. During Mrs. Dora's stay in Zabierzow the correspondence between Artur Biberstein and her was facilitated by the above two men who were also active outside of Zabierzow.

Once, *Rottenführer* (Corporal) Ritschek, well-known in the ghetto, while searching Artur, found in his possession an unfinished letter to Dora. He beat and arrested him. It appeared that this was the end. Vigorous intervention with *Sturmscharführer* (Major) Kunde led to his release. The intervening person was Dr. Weichert; because Artur worked in his office, he was miraculously saved. Probably no one could speak with the Germans as well as Dr. Weichert. He knew them well, understood their mentality and the way they reasoned. Many people owe their lives to him without even knowing it.

Occasionally, Dr. Romuald Lachs, a urologist, an excellent surgeon, tall, elegantly dressed, who spoke slowly and thoughtfully, visited the pharmacy. He left the impression that he was a man who could always solve problems. Regarding the situation of the Jews in the ghetto, and the fate that awaited them, he had from the very start an unalterable opinion. "They will perish, they have to, that's obvious, you only have to look at what's going on around you. I am waiting, for the time being," he said, "but I am not going to let them finish me off here!" On the day preceding one of the deportations, Dr. Lachs disappeared. No one knew anything specifically about it. Later, we learned that he managed to get to Warsaw with his family, and there he was taken prisoner during the Warsaw Uprising. He was herded with other rebels against the German tanks that were attacking the insurgent barricades. He died a hero.

Many diverse characters drifted through the pharmacy. Dr. Wiktor Kepler was a tall man, slightly stooped, with his head low, large black eyes, and a fixed smile on his face. He spoke in a soft voice. Choosing his words carefully he would look directly into the eyes of the listener. He was forty-five years old. He worked in the hospital in the department of internal diseases. He would never sit down; always standing he would repeat several times, "And what will happen to us? *Ich sehe schwarz* (I see black)." Unwilling to be separated from his wife, who was listed for the March deportation, he joined her voluntarily. One of the Germans, seeing him on the deportation square, pulled him out of the crowd. Kepler found himself in the Plaszow camp from where he was transferred to the one in Szebnia. During the liquidation of that camp before the end of the war, he was shot.

Dr. Jan Lachs, Assistant Professor at Jagiellonic University, a seventy-three-year-old gynecologist, was very active in spite of his age and eagerly participated in surgical operations which were always successful. He was an outstanding authority on the history of medicine, constantly poring over old folios which contained treasures of medical science of past centuries. There was a procedure, commonly used in the ghetto and recommended by him, which, when applied over several months, made it impossible to detect the presence of a past circumcision.

Several times during the ghetto's existence, the pharmacy was visited by Mr. Salomon Spitzer, authoritative orientalist, who was also a teacher of Jewish religion in the *Gymnasium* (high school) of Podgorze, which I frequented.

And finally, I must include a very well-known and highly respected personality, Dr. Aleksander Biberstein, the manager of the hospital for infectious diseases in the ghetto. This hospital was originally located on Rekawka Street and later moved to the dead-end, little street off Plac Zgody. Dr. Biberstein was a prominent diagnostician, an excellent organizer, socially active, and an exceptional human being who was known not only in Podgorze, but also in all Cracow for many years before the war. He lived in the ghetto with his wife and son. My friendship with Dr. Biberstein dated back many years before the war. Strangely, it happened that we did not meet in the ghetto very frequently, but this was understandable since we did not lead normal lives. Constant lack of time, worry about earning a living, and a tremendous amount of work, which burdened all doctors and especially Dr. Biberstein, did not provide an environment for much social life. For many years, until his departure for Israel, he held the position of the director of the social security organization in Cracow. I maintained contact with him through correspondence until the end of his life.

Many people passed through my pharmacy during this period as friends, acquaintances, or as strangers who were more or less interesting. It would be impossible to list all the names of those who deserve at least a few lines of remembrance. They would doubtless include many potentially interesting persons with whom the opportunity for closer relationships was precluded.

CHAPTER 2

—Still Peaceful—
The First Deportation
—German Confidants—
Deportations Two to Four
—June 1942—

Time passed rapidly in the constant bustle of the pharmacy, which was in continuous operation night and day for almost two years—in the company of close or casual friends and acquaintances. We shared, with the inhabitants of the ghetto, their sorrows and worries, keenly interested in each regulation of the occupying and local authorities. After each major incident and deportation, our friends and acquaintances came to the pharmacy. I was seldom there alone, especially after the curfew hour. Many people, who were afraid of being arrested, spent the night with me. They left the pharmacy in the early morning hours through the rear of the building. After the deportation actions, we rejoiced with all who remained. We would drink for good luck, to quiet the crying, and to deaden the pain of those who suffered a cruel fate. Then we would find out who was gone, who was wounded, who perished, and who lost their dear ones. Here were related many tales about fateful occurrences, miraculous coincidences resulting in the good or bad luck of various people. Every one would excitedly describe his own experiences, offer his opinions on many facets of the action, and praise or complain about some particular OD men.

Occasionally non-Jews would come into the ghetto. Among them was Dr. Ludwig Zurowski, a physician. He was allowed to enter because he was a city health commissioner. He took advantage of this privilege to bring food, mainly fats, and . . . he "rejuvenated" Jews by supplying them with hair dyes. The old and gray who were considered useless for labor and were therefore most in danger of extermination became, due to the proper cosmetics, *arbeitsfähig* (fit for work). Hundreds of liters of liquid, which removed the grayness, restoring the original hair color, left the pharmacy laboratory.

My colleague from the Gymnasium, attorney Mgr. Mieczyslaw Kossek, was a frequent guest in the pharmacy, and when I collected materials for my memoirs, he gave me a report entitled "A Meeting in the Pharmacy." I quote this portion:

> When I went to court in Podgorze for the first time, I found myself in the middle of the ghetto and I was overcome by a strange, disagreeable feeling of anxiety, sadness, and a deep sympathy for a people who had to suffer so cruelly. I saw a group of children, pale and emaciated, jumping on one leg, playing hopscotch; seeing a stranger, perhaps German, they stopped playing and looked at me apprehensively, wondering how I would treat them. I gave them some candies that I had with me for treating the secretaries in the court. I left because the start of the court proceedings was drawing close. The court building was at Czarniecki Street No. 3, in the ghetto area. I passed the pharmacy "Under the Eagle." Since I was in a hurry I did not enter. After the court proceedings, I stopped in and, not believing my own eyes, I saw my colleague, Tadeusz Pankiewicz, in a white apron. We spoke for a long time.
>
> Since then (it was the year 1941), several times a week, whenever I had court proceedings, I would stop at the pharmacy where other colleagues came and we chatted and exchanged news from the BBC and the underground papers.
>
> Then we agreed on how we could facilitate the exodus of the Jews from the ghetto. Periodically we would furnish Pankiewicz with two or three civil court summonses by means of which the Jews were permitted, by the German guards, to leave the ghetto.
>
> These court summonses had valid signatures, prepared by the court secretaries, Aleksandra Wysocka and Mieczyslawa Kobylarz. Space was left only for the first and family name of the summoned, which Pankiewicz filled in as needed. In this manner many persons left the ghetto.

On the way to the court or coming from it, Antoni Wronski, a teacher in Podgorze, would drop in. Before the war, he and Boleslaw Taszycki, the father of the well-known linguist Witold, would come to my father's pharmacy for herb medications almost every day. Very popular in Podgorze, Prof. Wronski, a charming man, who the students called "Goatee," brought cigarettes and distributed them to the prisoners in the court jail where he taught illiterates voluntarily. Once he came to me and, handing me a little note, he said, "Tadeusz dear, what are these characters doing? Is it not enough that they stole the cigarettes from my pocket, which were destined for them anyway, they also make jokes." On the note was written, "Professor, thanks for the fags. Please bring some vodka, as well. Then we will learn better!"

Occasionally I would meet Dr. Jozef Wronski, son of Professor Wronski, who organized secret Gymnasium classes in the proletarian neighborhoods of Podgorze, because it was known that the Germans liquidated all the Gymnasia in the occupied territory.

Three ladies worked with me, Mgr. Irena Drozdzikowska, Mgr. Helena Krywaniuk, and Mgr. Aurelia Danek-Czortkowa, who, from the very beginning in the ghetto, involved themselves in the ongoing effort to help the confined. As long as the Jews could leave the ghetto by showing a pass, they took care of most of their personal affairs. As soon as the ghetto was closed, and the individual departures were stopped, the role of the three ladies became significant. They took care of applications, delivered correspondence, became intermediaries in various affairs between Polish acquaintances living outside the ghetto and the Jews, purchased food, bought presents which were necessary for the Jews for various purposes. They also provided difficult-to-obtain medications frequently smuggled out of the Reich, and brought in small objects hidden with the Polish people by Jews when they left Cracow to live in the ghetto. Many Jews, who could not know what the living conditions would be like in the ghetto, or whether they would be subjected to searches, left valuables and money with Polish friends for safe keeping. As it was proved later on, many could better withstand the difficult periods in the ghetto and the Plaszow camp and even in the camps located much further beyond the Cracow area thanks to the monies and other valuable objects deposited by them outside of the ghetto. An intermediary in all of this was Dr. M. Weichert, who was the Head of the ZSS (Jewish Social Self-Help), and who had access to various small camps located outside of the ghetto and Plaszow area.

It was well known that this kind of help, transferring scrip or valuable objects, was quite dangerous.

I must say, without exaggeration, that we were well liked by everybody, and that during the entire time of our ghetto existence, we did not have a single argument, unpleasantness, or trouble with the ghetto inhabitants.

We were met at every step with signs of overwhelming and perhaps even unjustified gratitude. Many letters from camps and, after liberation, from different countries of Europe, came and continued to come to prove that the ties of empathy knotted during the common life in the ghetto were permanent.

In the first weeks of the ghetto's existence, the pharmacy was closed on some Sundays. (The directive ordering the pharmacy to be open continually day and night, regardless of holidays and Sundays, was published eight months after the establishment of the ghetto.) This permitted the ghetto dwellers to apply for passes for leaving in order to go to another pharmacy. During that time, our certification on the prescription that the prescribed medication was not available was sufficient justification for obtaining a pass to leave the ghetto. We gave this notation to anyone who asked for it.

On those free Sundays, I would occasionally go with friends to a coffeehouse on Limanowska Street which was well-known for their fine grain coffee and excellent homemade pastries. One could eat very well at the restaurant next to the gate on Limanowska Street. Stuffed derma with farfel, gefilte fish, and chulent on Saturdays—all these were specialties of the ghetto kitchen. On warm, sunny Sundays, people would walk and, after work, get some fresh air, to give them a fleeting taste of freedom on the tiny square at Jozefinska Street right next to the OD or on the slopes of the Krzemonki Hills, a very tiny piece of which was within the ghetto.

At that time, the ghetto experienced a small sensation. We found out one evening that Dr. Edmund Rosenhauch, the well-known Cracow ophthalmologist, was brought here. He took an apartment on Plac Zgody. He was kept there under house arrest, guarded by an OD man, and was not allowed to go anywhere. It was rumored that SS General Kruger was to visit him as a private patient. The expected visit, however, did not materialize. Dr. Rosenhauch disappeared mysteriously from the ghetto. Later on, we heard that he left for Warsaw and there survived the occupation in hiding, disguised as a monk in one of the monasteries of the capital. The flight of Rosenhauch and his trip to Warsaw were supposed to have been arranged by Förster.

In the fall of 1941, surrounding communities were included in the town of Cracow, and therefore all the Jews who lived in these areas had to move immediately to the Cracow ghetto. I remember, as if it were only yesterday, that the Day of Atonement, the holiest day of the Jewish calendar, was designated as the last day for moving. The German proclivity for viciousness was limitless. That evening was exceptionally cold and rainy. Scores of people, freezing, with small children, surrounded by heaps of packages and pots and pans, waited for permission to enter the ghetto, which was already overcrowded. The population was estimated at 17,000.

Life moved oddly. From the very early morning hours people congregated in front of the gates, preparing to go to work. Only the nonworkers, the sick and the old, were left behind. In the evening, the ghetto would be teeming with people who stood still or walked about in groups, conversing and commenting on the latest news from the front, and shopping. The restaurants and cafés were full. Street trade flourished; cigarettes, sandwiches, and cookies sold briskly.

And so each day that passed was the same as another. People adapted to the new conditions; they even started to believe that in this manner it would be possible to endure, as long as things remained the same—as long as conditions did not become worse. Weeks, then months, passed . . .

One morning the Germans issued an order to remove approximately 1,000 people because the ghetto was overcrowded. First, the old and the unemployed had to be removed. The Judenrat, together with the OD, were assigned to carry out this action.

Implementation of the first of the major tasks became the responsibility of Symche Spira. This man, blindly dedicated to the Germans, carried out with the utmost precision every German order and recommendation. He would guess and anticipate their thinking, exceed them in their eagerness, and impress them with his unquestioning zeal. Their commands were important to him, nothing else mattered. Symche Spira was a megalomaniac, wrapped in fantasy, a classic example of a psychopath, neurotic, bilious, suffering frequent attacks of gallstones, an erotic individual constantly looking for new easy amorous adventures, semi-illiterate, spoke Polish and German poorly, a human machine, an unthinking robot, carrying out the Gestapo orders as if hypnotized. He had a personal secretary who was also one of his girlfriends.

Spira got to work on the German order. The news about the directive spread with lightning speed throughout the ghetto, to every apartment and to every corner. Fear and anxiety overcame the people. OD prepared lists of names and at night pulled victims from their beds and their homes and led them to the station. The next morning, they checked over their papers and verified their places of employment. If it appeared that one was not working, he was held and transferred to the courtyard of the OD. The German regulation ordered that these people be relocated to other areas. Not everyone believed that. In the pharmacy, there was uncertainty and worry.

We spent the night with many of our acquaintances who preferred to be outside of their own homes because it wasn't known whether there would be new arrests that night.

This was a strange night. Virtually no one could even nap. Before morning, people silently left the pharmacy through the rear door and through the courtyard of the lab, singly and at irregular intervals. Danger lurked on every street corner; any conversation louder than a whisper at this early hour, or any group of people walking together, aroused suspicion and interest.

On the next morning, at about ten o'clock, the streets of the ghetto appeared strange. People huddled in groups on corners, commenting on the regulation and discussing what was about to happen. All eyes were directed toward the OD yard from whence the column of those going into the unknown was about to move.

They go! The crowd carried the terrible news ever farther. They came out of the apartment houses, opened the windows—whoever was in the ghetto watched what was going on in the streets. Fixed, semi-deranged stares followed the procession of the deportees. They marched through Targowa Street, through the Plac Zgody toward Plaszow. Old people, women and men, children—all marched together. On their backs they carried their most precious possessions, the belongings they considered the most necessary on their way into the unknown and uncertain future. Beside them marched the OD. The silence was unearthly. Nobody screamed at anyone. Nobody beat anyone. Like a funeral procession, they moved toward the ghetto exit. Those watching, friends, relatives, and acquaintances, did so with eyes dulled by pain and terror. They were gone. Only the cries of those left behind, and the futile hope of seeing them again, remained.

At the railroad station in Plaszow the deportees were loaded into freight cars and given bread for the road. (The ghetto bakeries had baked it the previous night, at the expense of the community!) The train carried them several hundred kilometers to the district of Lublin. At the predetermined point, the train stopped, the doors of the cars were opened, and the people were forced to leave. They were ordered to scatter to the nearby settlements. Dumbfounded, they had only one desire—to return as quickly as possible to the ghetto, to their dear ones, in spite of the threats of the death penalty for those returning to Cracow.

Some, after several days, others, after several weeks, were back in the ghetto. They used whatever means possible. Some removed their armbands, risking heavy penalties for disobeying the regulations; others boarded trains or used carts or private cars, even military ones, and the rest walked.

From time to time people would disappear from the ghetto in this fashion: a list was prepared by a Jewish Gestapo agent, Szymon Szpic, in cooperation with the OD Commander Spira; using this list the suspects were pulled from their homes, usually at night, and delivered to the OD so that they could be transported early in the morning by German cars under heavy police guard, either to Pomorska Street or in an unknown direction where all traces of them disappeared. There were many such cases. Jews disappeared and, also at the outset, some Poles who operated various enterprises in the ghetto. Even I was included on one of those lists. However, before it was sent out, the news reached Dr. Blau, the physician, and thanks to her efforts, and also those of some of my other acquaintances, the author of the list, Szpic, was persuaded to delete my name. The charge against me was that during the night many of the ghetto inhabitants constantly gathered in my pharmacy. This was told to me some months later by the charming Dr. Blau.

Dr. Blau's intervention saved my life at that time. She had a younger brother, Carlos, in the ghetto, who vaguely remembered me from the pharmacy. After he lost his parents and his sister and the physician was murdered, he was imprisoned in a German camp. The end of the war brought him freedom. After many hardships, he left Poland, and later Europe, to settle in distant Costa Rica. He became a successful entrepreneur, a rich man, and married a very charming and impressive Spanish lady. They had several children and were very happy. He found my address and wrote me a long, warm letter in which he introduced himself, reminiscing about Cracow, the house where he was born, and the streets where he played. His parents told him a great deal about my pharmacy. So many years after he left Poland, he still spoke and wrote Polish flawlessly. He had already visited Cracow twice with his wife. They liked everything—they were excited about it all. I spent some unforgettable hours with them. They told me, and they repeated this in writing constantly, that although they had no close friends or acquaintances in Cracow, they came to visit me. How moving it was to hear these words after so many years. We corresponded a great deal, and I eagerly await the opportunity to meet with them again.

A similar thing happened to me in the year 1959 when I received a letter from Hirsch Pariser, who also knew me only slightly. He was the son of a very wealthy man who, together with his relatives, owned tremendous warehouses of flour, barley, rice, and other agricultural products, at the Vistula embankment. The company name was "Dranger-Pariser, Agricultural Warehouses." Hirsch Pariser was in the ghetto when he was very young. After he lost his parents, he was transported from the ghetto to a German camp. Finally the war was over, and with its end came the longed-for freedom. Young Hirsch Pariser settled permanently in Belgium, married, and had two sons. In his first letter he described the tragedies he experienced in the ghetto, the death of his beloved parents and relatives, his own misfortunes in the German camps, and his liberation at the very last moment. He invited me to visit with deep sincerity, "Please come—my wife and I would be very happy." I spent a whole month in their charming villa. At night we reminisced about the old times. My stay with the Parisers was a very moving experience. So much kindness, so much friendship shown to me by my hosts; I shall remember with deep gratitude, their warm hospitality.

I had many kindred experiences. Young people searched out my address many years after the war just to send me a few kind words . . .

Who was this Szpic, who placed me on the list to be arrested? He was a man of about fifty-five years, drawn, slender, tall, swarthy faced, slightly stooped, with a fixed sneering smile on his face, he was known in Cracow before the war because of his notorious court trial for fraud and swindling people out of their money by falsely promising to find them employment. He was sentenced to several years in prison. He was the terror of the ghetto—pity the man who started a quarrel with him—his days would be numbered! Szpic died at the hands of the Gestapo, as did all of those who served them. Together with another Gestapo spy, Bialobroda, he was sent to the vicinity of Radom purportedly to search for dissidents who were active there. Sometime later, news reached us that both of them were killed. The Germans confirmed this. It then became quite clear that this was how the Hitlerites paid for the servile work of the traitors.

Using similar lists, many young people were arrested. Among them was the above mentioned Maryla Schenker. A German personally came to pick her up. Entering the apartment of her parents at Jozefinska Street he asked her mother, "Wo ist diese schöne Blonde?" (Where is that pretty blonde?) When Miss Schenker appeared, he took a long look at her and said, "Ach, du bist diese schöne. Nun gut, komm mit." (Ah, you are that pretty one. Very good, come with me.)

She went with him to the OD and then she was transported to Auschwitz, where she died of pneumonia. I remember how much trouble her father had and how much money, and the extensive efforts he expended to save her. One German undertook to intervene in her behalf. He found another SS man who, for a certain sum of money, was supposed to facilitate her flight to Holland where she had close relatives. He received part of the money as a down payment; he was to get the balance when the relatives confirmed in writing that Miss Maryla was with them. After a while, this SS man produced a letter in Miss Schenker's handwriting. She wrote that she was in Holland, that she was healthy and happy. Several weeks later, a letter was received from the relatives in which there was not even a mention of the girl. The deceit of the German became obvious, particularly when a card from Auschwitz arrived a few days later in which the daughter wrote: "I am healthy and doing well."

Aside from Szpic, I should mention some other informers who carried on their activities both in the ghetto and beyond its walls, and to whom the Germans assigned various functions. Among them were Julek Appel, the aforementioned Bialobroda, Stefania Brandstatter or Poklewska, Chilowicz and his wife, Finkelstein, Förster, Marcel Gruner, Marcel Goldberg, Kleinberger, Kerner, Michal Pacanower, Szymon Rosen, Marian Rotkopf, Ignacy Traubmann, Weininger, Weismann, and many others about whom we did not have positive proof. These informers infiltrated all the institutions of the ghetto, including the customs house. Brodman and Steinfeld were particularly useful to the Germans there. We kept the names of the informers on prescription blanks which I kept hidden during the occupation. Virtually all of them perished at the hands of the Gestapo or Polish underground organizations.

A very dangerous couple in the service of the Gestapo was the Selingers. He was of medium height, brown-haired, carefully groomed, and well-dressed; and she, petite, bleached blond hair, a doll-like beauty, who spoke poor Polish. They collaborated with the Obersturmführer Theodore Heinemayer, who was counselor of the Gestapo for political affairs. In the cafés she would eavesdrop on the conversations of the Germans; he would not slight any task assigned to him by the Gestapo. He denounced Jews who had Aryan papers and Poles who were in contact with the Jews.

The ultimate fate of the Selingers throws an important light on the cynicism of the Germans. Selinger, realizing that sooner or later he would die in the same way as the other informers, decided to check out the situation in Hungary, where many others sought escape. First he went to the border by himself; a week later he returned to take his wife. Then he was called on by Theodore Heinemayer, who knew everything.

"If you want to run away, then don't be stupid and don't take risks, because if you are caught at the frontier, then nothing will help you. If you wish, I'll give you a letter to the chief of police in Nowy Targ, who will help you to escape. I simply want to help you. You did a lot for me; I should like to prove to you that Germans are decent people."

Selinger did not know how to thank him. Heinemayer wrote a letter and handed it to the informer. A few days later, the Selingers left for Nowy Targ. There they reported to the chief of police and handed over the letter of recommendation. The German took the letter and asked them to sit down. After all, the letter was not from just anybody, it was from Heinemayer himself. After reading it, he asked them to come with him to the courtyard; there he read the letter to them. Heinemayer ordered the carriers shot. Heinemayer's "recommendation" was carried out. Later it was learned that only Mrs. Selinger perished; he survived to the end of the war. How is not known. After the war he appeared in Cracow—later he supposedly went to America.

This story was related to me by the assistant commander of Schupo, Bousko, and he in turn heard it at a Gestapo party where Heinemayer bragged about how he wanted to test the wits of Selinger. He reasoned: "If he is smart, he will open the letter and after reading it, he will run away. If he doesn't open it, then he deserves his fate." In another version of this story, Selinger became aware of the contents of the letter, and with his wife, escaped to Hungary.

In 1978, I was a witness at a trial against Heinemayer in Hanover. I sat face to face with the accused. He was elderly, stout, with a pleasant manner, responding to the court with an air of confidence, and in no way resembling the terrible Heinemayer of the ghetto days. For four hours during the examination of the witnesses, he remained almost motionless, staring before him as if he were under a spell. He was found not guilty.

The atmosphere in the ghetto, in spite of the apparent calm, was getting worse. Constant conferences between the Judenrat and the German authorities on the topic of overcrowding in the ghetto area, which had to be brought down, created anxiety. The word "deportation" was not mentioned directly, but people began to speculate and guess that something evil was about to happen. The uncertainty worried them and disturbed their peace of mind.

The suspicions and forebodings proved correct in June 1943. The ghetto was surrounded during the night by a strong cordon of *Sonderdienst* (Special Police). Guards were posted around the barbed-wire fences. No one from outside could approach the ghetto boundaries. Jews whose windows faced the Aryan area were forbidden to show themselves there, to open them, or appear on the balconies. Those who disobeyed were likely to be shot. Germans would shoot into the windows as soon as they spotted anyone.

Panic gripped the ghetto. Deportation and its implications dominated all conversations. Who will go and who will remain? Nothing could be known for a certainty. The Germans did not reveal their plans. No one dared ask. Besides, all of their answers were lies!

On the 29th, 30th, and 31st of May, various commissions met in the buildings of the ZSS (Jewish Social Self-Help). The Gestapo and officials of the labor office participated in these meetings. Small tables were set up in the large hall of the former building of the savings bank. At each table sat a Gestapo man and an official of the labor office, and a long line of people faced them, trembling, about to hear their fate. Outside of the building, crowds gathered in lines extending for several blocks. The Gestapo decided, there and then, who would remain and who would leave the ghetto. People who did not receive permission to stay asked with fear, "Where will they send us? Will they let us take anything along?" They tried to calm each other as best they could. No one really believed in outright perdition, and no one yet dreamed about crematoriums, poison gas, or burning human pyres. For the first time, rumors began to circulate about what the Germans had supposedly decided in deepest secrecy about open labor camps in the Ukraine where the deported would work in the fields. The German railroaders spoke about the tremendous barracks that were awaiting the transports, about the life organized in those newly erected barrack towns where there were restaurants, libraries, and cinemas, accessible to all. They said that the working Jews were being paid and that they would be able to live there through the war in peace and quiet. People started to believe. A new worry: how about the food? Would it be possible to take along large amounts of provisions? On the other hand, people tried by all means possible to obtain from the SS or the police commandant an official stamp on their identity cards allowing them to remain. No one guessed then that this stamp would decide the difference between life and death.

The decision would be made at the whim of one German: the work certificate or the type of work one could do were not the determining factors. These were paradoxical situations: someone who was refused a stamp could be returned to the very same table and an hour later receive the stamp without any difficulties. Someone else who was refused a stamp at one table could receive it at the next one. Coincidence, luck, the mood of the Gestapo man or his caprice, the importance of the sponsor, the sum of money offered, the clarity and size of the diamond for trade—these were the determinants that decided whether one was deported or remained in the ghetto. The registration was completed within two days. People without stamps on their passes prayerfully awaited their fate.

On the 1st of June 1942, the OD was ordered to bring from their apartments to Plac Zgody all those who did not have the stamp. At night the OD went through all the houses and reviewed the identity cards. Those destined for deportation were detained. The same procedure took place in the early morning of the next day. The pharmacy was occupied again with acquaintances who called during the night.

At daybreak on June 2nd, as in a nightmare, like specters from the grave, crawled a procession of men and women. They were mostly old people, but there was no lack of the young among them. Many were children from whom the parents refused to part.

Like apparitions in a horror novel, they moved with faltering steps, carrying all their possessions on their weary backs, as heavy as the tragic burden of the fate they were facing.

The Plac Zgody filled up slowly with people and their packages, bundles, valises, and all kinds of luggage. The searing sun burned. A sweltering day lay ahead. Thirst dried the throat, frazzled nerves were stretched to the limit. Fear, terror, and madness could be seen in their eyes.

Through the entry gate from the Plac Zgody, two cars entered and stopped about 150 feet from my pharmacy. Two Gestapo men got out of the first car; one of them approached the man sitting in the second car, then the second car proceeded in the direction of the OD.

I opened the pharmacy that day at the same time I did on any other day. From deep inside I watched. What was going to happen? What was actually happening? After a short while, I saw that the two Gestapo men who remained on Plac Zgody pulled revolvers out of their holsters, cocked the triggers, and with slow deliberate steps approached the pharmacy. The crunch of their boots could be heard clearly from the square, which was ominously silent. I did not understand a thing—I looked at my ladies wonderingly—we exchanged a few remarks on what was happening here before our eyes. We could not understand—what it was for—or against whom? We were living through a dramatically unique moment. Just then the door opened and the two Germans entered. They were both tall and handsome, attired in perfectly tailored Sonderdienst uniforms, hats on their heads with dull emblems of the skull and crossbones. Without a word of greeting, they approached the ladies. I asked, "You wish . . . ?"—I did not receive an answer. Their steely penetrating gaze moved slowly over our faces, then at the pharmacy equipment, the medications, touching each item, moving down the wall, stopping momentarily at each holy picture illuminated by a small lamp, to return again to me and my personnel . . .

the silence was deathlike. After a moment and without a word, they placed their revolvers on the marble counter, and loaded the guns. The metal sound of the bullets being inserted into the chambers filled the room. They cocked the triggers again. A wry smile quickly crossed their faces and they left, again without a word. All this was incomprehensible to me!

The streets leading to the Plac Zgody were emptying out. People were hiding in the building entranceways. Spira, with his entire personal staff, ran around like a madman. The Gestapo officers left the pharmacy and the door closed behind them. We saw one of them slowly aiming his revolver in the direction of Jozefinska Street. The OD men called each other. Then a shot . . . one . . . a second . . . a third! And then slowly the smoking pistol was lowered. The voices were stilled. Only the fast footsteps of the running OD men broke the eerie silence. Why did he shoot? At whom did he aim? Did he hit anyone? Was this perhaps only a scare? These were the thoughts and questions that quickly crossed my mind. We later learned there was a man wounded, but, fortunately, not fatally. The first Gestapo man to shoot in the ghetto was SS Sturmscharführer Kriminalsekretar Wilhelm Kunde, assigned to Jewish affairs in the Sicherheitspolizei. The first one wounded was Dr. Weichert, the President of the Jewish Social Self-Help. The bullet ricocheted and hit him in the arm.

More new cars drove in, and more new Gestapo men appeared in the ghetto. A variety of uniforms and ranks could be seen. Representatives of different military and police divisions, officials of various departments of the city authority appeared—to fill their eyes with the unusual sight.

New groups of Jews kept coming to the Plac Zgody. The crowd grew slowly until it filled all the empty space. At first the people stood. After a while, they sat on the ground or on their bundles. The sun burned mercilessly and parched their throats. Across the street from the pharmacy, under the wall of an apartment house, doctors, nurses, hospital sisters in white coats, and technicians with stretchers were gathered. The white of the doctors' coats contrasted strangely with the black and gray of the crowd waiting for deportation. The door of the pharmacy was constantly opened. These were the doctors, hospital sisters, and OD men taking medications for those to be deported. Valerian drops, bromides, sedatives, and heart medicines were our last gifts to the departing. The crowd stood or sat—waiting in fear and uncertainty.

Open trucks and carriages entered the Plac Zgody. The deportees ran toward them, rushing to find a seat and a place for their luggage. The throng pushed. Age and strength determined who got there first. In a few minutes

Jewish evacuation from Cracow in 1942

all the carts were filled, jammed with people and their belongings. The SS men looked at the turmoil with jeering smiles. For the second time that day, the door of the pharmacy was opened by a member of the Gestapo. Two young fellows, about 26 years old, entered. This time with a greeting: "Good Morning!" They asked whose pharmacy this was and how one could get to the balcony. I explained. They thanked us and left. From the balcony they took photographs to show to the world the humaneness of the Germans in treating the "deportees" or rather the "resettled." It should be noted that the word "deportees" was not allowed and similarly "Jewish Quarter" replaced the word "ghetto."

The click of the cameras—the cranking of the film in the professional Leicas—and the propaganda swindle was done! It could be shown throughout the world; it would become an important document one day. And the people waited. The heat was brutal—some collapsed from fatigue, many fainted. Then came a short command. "Alle Heraus! Schnell—Raus!" (Everybody out! Quickly—out!). How terrifying this sounded. In the blink of an eye, the carts were emptied. The Germans, and on their orders, the OD men, threw down the valises and luggage, pulled off the old people and pushed the younger ones down, just to hurry the process. People looked with terror at one another—what did all this mean? Was all this action with the carts a ploy to make a propaganda film?

To the terrifying yells of the Germans, the crowd arose, sat down, got up again, waving, huddled ever so much closer. At first slowly, then faster, finally running, constantly being pushed, beaten and driven by Germans howling inarticulately, the crowd left the Plac Zgody, the heavy baggage borne agonizingly. Some dropped the heavier pieces; the SS men seized bundles from others. Along the trolley tracks toward Plaszow, the crowd crawled. The assassins screamed ever more loudly—"Raus, raus, los, schnell!" These words harassed the people during all of the occupation; they were heard everywhere—and continually. The maltreated exiles fell to the ground, bleeding, arose only to fall again, dropping the bundles from their bloodied hands. Some didn't pick them up. Why should they be burdened with them on their way to death? Sometime later, the square was empty—carts loaded with bread entered. This was the last gift the deportees received from the remaining population. (At the recommendation of the Judenrat, bread was baked in all of the bakeries during the preceding night.) Desolation and quiet. In the square, which was filled with people a short while ago, there remained only packages and bundles, and here and there prayer books wrapped in velvet. Those who remained could not believe that everything they saw had really happened. The shock was numbing. The horror deprived them of arriving at an objective grasp of the facts.

Following the deportees, the German dignitaries left by car, as well as the SS and Gestapo men of the higher ranks. Only the counselors for Jewish affairs remained. After two hours even they left. But the walls were still surrounded by the many guard posts: this was an obvious sign that the Aktion for this day was not finished yet. A terrible night fell, during which very few could close their eyes. The uncertainty of tomorrow for those who remained, their despair, their feeling of helplessness against the brutal outrage broke their spirit. Many people were in the pharmacy that night. They constantly watched the clock on the wall. Its hands did not seem to move. No one slept. Everyone waited.

Some of those who were refused the rubber stamps, or who stopped trying and left their fortune to fate, but who did not report for the first deportation, now tried, by all possible means, to change the decisions of the Germans. The ghetto telephones worked overtime; conversations with the bosses of the various posts where Jews were employed were carried on incessantly. In many cases, such intervention brought the desired result. The executives either came down personally, or attended to the problem by telephone, speaking with the officials of the labor department in the ghetto or eventually with the Gestapo men.

The Germans were not satisfied with the number deported. They calculated that many who did not have the stamps on their passes did not report.

An order was issued to review the documents of all the dwellers and to hold everyone who did not have a permit to remain in the ghetto. During the night, from the 3rd to the 4th of June 1942, the Gestapo, Sonderdienst, and OD men inspected papers, stopped and searched people on the streets, entered the hospitals and old age homes, searched the apartments and houses. There was no lack of beatings, stompings. This Aktion lasted till the morning of June 4. At dawn that day, large units of the Sonderdienst entered the ghetto in battle gear. Alongside them, the German police appeared, and for the first time, a detachment of Polish police in blue, and a detail of Polish farmers, forcibly recruited into the so-called "Baudienst." The German police aligned themselves at the apartment houses on Plac Zgody. Before them were ranged racks containing rifles, and behind them, just in front of the pharmacy windows, were stationed the Baudienst. Across the square were the police and next to them in a little street were the Jewish doctors, hospital nurses, and orderlies with stretchers. It was possible, without much difficulty, to obtain the proper stamps on the passes or blue cards for the medical service. But, for how long? The group consisted of perhaps ten people. They were supposed to render assistance, according to the German order, to those who might faint.

The processing of the deportees started. The first of these unfortunates came to the Plac Zgody. Pushed, beaten, and kicked, they moved ahead slowly at a funeral pace, soberly—and with dignity. Others ran in groups, or singly—still others appeared dazed. They were surrounded by German policemen, who held their rifles with fingers on the trigger, ready to shoot. The crowd moved directly before my windows. The proceedings were accompanied by constant screaming, merciless beatings, and shootings. Many fell dead, and many were wounded and all this during the first moments of the deportation.

Before my eyes, as in a phantom kaleidoscope, moved unearthly scenes. The ghetto reverberated with shots. Soldiers were running amok with smoking rifles, officers with pistols, pokers, clubs, and whips. The corpses and wounded were removed by the hospital orderlies, making their way through the crowd under constant fire. The Germans shot as if possessed, at random, at whosoever satisfied their whim. Apparently, blood exacerbated their bestial and sadistic instincts.

In accordance with official German regulations, it was permitted to take all the luggage, which was not inspected on Plac Zgody in the first transport. This time the Germans carried out a detailed personal search either in Plac Zgody, before all eyes, or in the doorways or stores. The luggage was taken away as a rule, and the searches were accompanied by beatings and mayhem regardless of the age or sex of the victims.

I remember how, during that deportation, a pretty young woman burst into the pharmacy, running away from the crowd. She pushed through the gathered people, ran to the other rooms of the pharmacy, and disappeared from view. In the meantime, all kinds of strange things were happening to us: frequently somebody came in—we were given cards, requests for transmitting last instructions to their relatives, and changes in decisions. The beaten and wounded asked for help. In 1956, I received a letter from Israel from that young lady who reminded me about that incident in the pharmacy. She took advantage of the confusion and hid herself in the second room under one of the counters, waited there for a time and left through the rear exit to get to the building courtyard, from where, through an alley to the opposite building, she reached the next street. Her name was Irena Halpern and she came from a well-to-do merchant family. Her father was the owner of a fur company on Grodzka Street in Cracow. The parents were murdered during the October 1942 deportation. She got to the Plaszow camp from where she was resettled to the camp in Skarzysko, and she finally was interred in the camp in Czestochowa where she survived until the end of the war. After liberation she migrated to Israel. During my visit there, I enjoyed the generous hospitality of Irena and her husband.

Here and there, doctors, nurses, and ODs rushed into the pharmacy, taking medications and bandages for the beaten and wounded. I should like to mention modestly that we did not accept any payment for the sedatives, sleeping pills, pain medications, and bandages from those who were going to a certain death. The more seriously wounded were transferred to the hospital on Jozefinska Street.

New groups of people pulled from their hiding places were constantly entering the square. Like phantoms, in front of the pharmacy windows, old people, women, and children dragged past. I saw an old lady about 70, with windblown hair, walking some distance away from a large group of deportees; her eyes were glassy—unmoving—wide with fright—staring ahead. She walked slowly, calmly, wearing only a dress, shod in bedroom slippers; she had no luggage not even a purse. With both hands hugging her old woman's chest, she clutched something tiny and black. It was a little dog—she took only that which was most precious to her and with which she did not want to part.

A young girl passed by, smiling broadly, throwing her arms with indescribable movements, mentally ill, well-known to all ghetto dwellers, about 14 years old. She was barefoot, dressed only in a torn nightgown. The sight of this laughing and exhilarated girl among those falling and trembling with fear made one shudder. Old and young passed by, some of them dressed; others only in underwear, pulled out of bed just as they were found. Sick people, after major surgery and protracted illness, were forced to go. They ran, pushed by fear, bloodied, amidst the jeers and laughter of the soldiers.

From the apartment house at Plac Zgody 2, across from the pharmacy, came a blind man, well-known to many of the ghetto dwellers—an old man about 70, wearing black eyeglasses on sightless eyes that he lost when fighting with the Germans in 1914 on the Italian front. On his left arm he wore a band of yellow with three circles, a sign of blindness. He entered, led on one side by his son and on the other by his wife, holding his head high. "He is lucky that he cannot see. It will be easier for him to die," the nurse said. On his breast was pinned a military decoration which he received in the war. Perhaps this would gain him some consideration from the Germans? In the beginning, people thought along these lines.

Following him was a crippled old man, on crutches with only one leg. The Germans approached him. With slow dancing steps, one of them ran to the blind man and yelled horribly, "Schnell!" This encouraged the other soldiers to start a macabre game. Two SS men approached the man without the leg and, screaming, urged him to run; another crept from the rear and struck the crutch with his rifle butt. The man fell to the ground. The German shouted like a maniac, threatening with his gun. All this happened just behind the blind man who of course saw nothing but only heard the inhuman roars of the Germans and the moans of the wounded, interrupted by bursts of laughter. A German soldier approached the fallen cripple and helped him up. This aid was recorded by a German officer, who so eagerly photographed all the scenes of "The German Help with the Humanitarian Resettlement of the Jews." For a moment we thought that perhaps there was one human among the German assassins who could not stand the mistreatment of the defenseless and innocent people in the last hours of their lives. Unfortunately, there was no such man in the tragic history of the Cracow ghetto.

Once they had gleefully satisfied themselves with the sight of the one-legged man, they decided to play the same game with the blind war veteran. First they sent his son away, then his wife, then they tripped him and enjoyed his fall. This time they did not help him to get up; he had to do it by himself—propelled by the terrifying screams of the SS men around him. This torture was repeated several times; the sight was really shocking in its cruelty. It would be hard to guess what they enjoyed more: the physical pain they inflicted on the man falling down or the despair suffered by his wife and son standing helplessly by, silent in the face of this outrage.

It would be very difficult to describe each individual case, each variation of the German crimes and horror that occurred before our eyes. The particular episodes described only seemed to be similar in all cases. But in reality, each was different; although they all started with beating and kicking, they frequently ended in shooting. Each abuse had its own distinctive tragic characteristics.

The ghetto echoed with shots; the dead and wounded fell; blood marked the German crimes in the streets. There were more and more people in the square. The heat, as on previous days, was unbearable—fire seemed to fall from the sky. Water was unavailable, but even if it were, it was forbidden to the sufferers. People, weakened by heat and thirst, fainted and fell. In front of the pharmacy there was a small army car to which every few minutes the SS men brought valises filled with valuables taken during the searches of the deportees. They took everything from them: rings, wedding bands, gold and steel watches, cigarette cases and even lighters. Some of the unfortunates looked at those waiting their turn, resignation and apathy etched in their faces. These people were already beyond feeling.

In the pharmacy we learned who was killed and where, who committed suicide, where the wounded were taken, and the names of the victims. The hospitals were full; the doctors were dressing wounds and trying to save those who had tried to poison themselves. Many people, threatened with deportation, owed their lives to Dr. Biberstein, manager of the epidemic hospital located on Rekawka Street. This building was the hiding place of many people who were given white coats so that they would look like members of the hospital staff. Dr. Biberstein hoped that the Germans, fearing infection, would not enter the hospital. And this is what happened.

When will it end? This question worried everyone. I looked through the windows of the pharmacy, standing aside so as not to be seen. The Gestapo did not like their exterminations to be witnessed. During the deportations, the trolleys were stopped; not even the German cars were permitted to pass through the ghetto. I saw a group of SS dignitaries approaching the pharmacy. They halted in front of my door; I heard their voices and I was able to understand each word because, as usual, they shouted. They came quite close to the door, hiding in a small recess in the wall. They were dissatisfied with the small number of deportees and with the help of the Judenrat. They blamed the Judenrat president, whose name was continually mentioned. After a while, I heard the shout of one of the SS men and a whistle directed at the OD men stationed farther down on Targowa Street. Their running steps could be heard; among the others I saw Spira standing a short distance from the SS. He came to attention, saluted and received a curt order to immediately bring the president of the Judenrat, Dr. Artur Rosenzweig.

A man approximately 40 years old, slim, with a long dried-out face and with nervous movements, drew near the group of Germans. He spoke with them in excellent German rather freely. This was David Gutter. After a few minutes, Rosenzweig appeared. He walked slowly, wore no hat, and had slightly blown gray hair, an elderly man. He stopped in front of the Gestapo and SS men, bowing his head slightly. A moment of silence—and then from one of the SS men came these terrible words: "Rosenzweig—as of this moment, you are relieved of your position; the Aktion did not have satisfactory results with respect to the number or the manner of delivery of the people to the square. This is all your fault." He then hit Dr. Rosenzweig on the head. I watched this from a distance of two meters, horrified. Dr. Rosenzweig did not utter a single word, but again bowed his head and walked away. The Germans turned to Gutter and told him that he was responsible for everything from now on. "Jawohl," Gutter replied, standing at attention.

The ghetto had a new commissioner—because what other title could Gutter assume now? He was formerly a traveling salesman who sold magazines. An extremely nervous man, always rushing, with uncoordinated movements, clever, glib, energetic, and able to follow and execute German orders as well as Spira could, but he was much more intelligent and more critical. He had his own opinions and was capable, in rapid-fire conversations, of interjecting clever adages. This impressed many of his listeners. Being placed in such a "high position" by the Germans turned his head and he behaved like a megalomaniac just as Spira did before him. From the moment of his appointment he began to officiate with great zeal. During the Aktion he ran crazily from one group of Germans to another, shouting and gesticulating. Observing him, I admired his colossal physical stamina.

Dr. Rosenzweig was arrested along with all of his family immediately after he failed to attain the presidency. He was included in a group of deportees who were transported to Belzec, where he perished in a gas chamber. Undoubtedly he was not useful to the Germans. An exceptionally decent man, with an impeccable reputation, a lawyer by profession, he was able to reason and think critically. He was not overwhelmed by the honor thrust upon him by the Germans—it was a burden—as was any managerial position in those days, especially for a man of honor and dignity.

What was the judgment about Dr. Rosenzweig? It was claimed that he was too indifferent to the incidents when, without prejudging an issue, some reprieve could have been obtained. For example, it should have been possible—in the opinion of some—to save the doctors from deportation by intervention, and to release those who were already in the transport.

At the time, no one considered the consequences and outcome of such intervention. The president was reproached for lack of action and decisiveness and for his uncompromising attitude to the different reasoning of his closest collaborators. This was explained by his apathy, resignation, and his feeling of impotence against the superpower, negating his faith in the efficacy of any efforts. He would gladly have resigned his high position, but he realized the danger of such action.

The deportations started. The square was emptied slowly. Some left by truck, others marched, rushed by the shoving Germans. Pushed, kicked, and beaten, they ran through Lwowska and Wielicka Streets, toward Plaszow. Along the way, the escorting Sonderdienst guards shot those who could not

Jewish evacuation from Cracow in 1942

keep pace. Corpses lined the route of the deportees. Blood streamed on the pavement.

At the Plaszow railroad station they were all loaded into cattle cars spread with quicklime, and with small barred windows at the top. Approximately 120 people were crammed into each car and the doors were closed tightly; each one of these transport units was guarded by German police. It was forbidden to offer water or bread. The heat was suffocating. The train started.

Several people were saved from this transport—those who had locksmith tools with them broke out the bars of the windows and jumped off the train traveling at full speed. They risked hitting the power poles, falling under the wheels, and most certainly bullets from the watchful guards.

There were also those who broke out the floorboards, and when the train stopped at a station, slid to the ground. When the wheels moved they passed over them. The future fate of these escapees depended on their good luck.

A boy I knew related later that he jumped from the speeding train but was spotted. The convoy guards shot and wounded him. He lost consciousness, rolled down the embankment and lay there for an undetermined time. When he woke, it was dark and raining. He crawled for several hours until he reached the first farmhouse, and so he dragged himself from house to house for days on end; the door did not always open for him; nor did he always hear a warm word of sympathy; not too often was he treated to some food. However, no one denounced him. He walked ahead for weeks. Time was healing the wound. He returned to the ghetto and remained there till March 13, 1943, the ghetto's final liquidation date.

During the above described deportation, I received another visit from SS Sturmführer Kunde, a counselor for Jewish affairs, who on the counter of my pharmacy was stamping the Kennkarten of the people protected by Spira and Förster.

With regard to Kunde, I was reminded of the following incident, so characteristic of the German mind, which is sometimes absolutely incomprehensible. When he walked through the streets, he was considered one who was very easy to approach, as was his colleague SS Obersturmführer Heinrich, who was also a counselor for Jewish affairs, both were reputed to be less brutal and were vulnerable to certain "arguments." Kunde was completely surrounded by people who begged him for the stamps. He was there for quite a while and talked with them—and the throng around him became tighter and tighter. Suddenly he spotted an approaching German on the other side of the street, and, fearful of being seen talking with Jews, he took out his revolver and threatened to shoot, and actually did once; the bullet ricocheted off the ground and wounded the lady physician Dr. Silberger. The crowd scattered in panic. A little girl of twelve fearfully scrambled away. Kunde started after her at full speed, caught up with her and asked her the reason for her flight; a man who happened to be nearby served as an interpreter. The girl stammered with dread, terrified that he would shoot her. "And what would you like from me?" he asked. "A stamp for my Daddy and Mommy," she answered. "And what are your parents?"—"My father is a shoemaker."

Kunde asked the child to bring the Kennkarten of the whole family, and stamped them in the pharmacy. We exploited this moment to obtain stamps for many other people who quite accidentally found themselves in the pharmacy. The ladies certainly knew how to take advantage of Kunde's good mood. In such hands were entrusted the lives of thousands of people, and often similar caprices decided their fate.

The ghetto was still surrounded by the Sonderdienst. German police leisurely patrolled the streets. From time to time, the guards touring the ghetto would shoot, particularly from Krzemionki, from where the whole Jewish quarter was clearly visible. And in the distance, beyond the Vistula, one could see Cracow with the tall hill of Wawel on whose steeple flew the hated flag with the swastika.

CHAPTER 3

—LIEUTENANT BOUSKO— DEPORTATION OF JUNE 8, 1942 —REDUCING THE SIZE OF THE GHETTO— DIFFICULT CONDITIONS OF LIFE —DEPORTATION OF OCTOBER 28, 1942— THE ATTITUDES OF THE PERSECUTORS

During the June Aktion, a strange figure appeared in the ghetto. This was the assistant to the German police commander in Podgorze, Lieutenant Oswald Bousko, a Viennese.

After two days of sitting uninterruptedly in the pharmacy, I went out beyond the ghetto in spite of the warning of one of the old German policemen that I would be in danger of being shot. "These people," he said, "do not care about anything—they do not care that you are an Aryan and that you have permission to stay in the ghetto: in the ghetto they can do whatever they want with impunity." I did not listen. I went. I walked through the streets, I passed the German police posts. The Germans looked at me with some curiosity; not seeing an armband on my sleeve, they apparently took me for a German, and did not stop me until I reached the exit gate. I went out; before me was a tall German about forty years old, blonde, with a lean face, light brown eyes, and a characteristic grimace at the corner of his mouth. He stared at me, in astonishment—he bent down and looked into my eyes. He asked for papers. I handed them over; he examined them and after a while returned them to me and began to revile me. He did not shout, he screamed! I did not understand what he wanted of me because he spoke a Viennese dialect. Finally I guessed what it was all about: he was concerned that I left the ghetto without a German police escort. He said that they could shoot me on the spot. I could not understand why he was so interested in my life. I wondered and I listened . . . He advised me that in the future if I wanted to go out, to call the station and he would send a police escort. I was amazed at his concern, particularly since he did not know me.

In spite of the terrible screams and abuse, I felt some empathy (if it could be called that!) man to man. For these times, this was quite a lot. Who was this policeman? His name was Bousko. In time I found out many interesting details about him. He was born in Vienna, the son of a low-grade official. As a teenager he was placed in a monastery to become a brother. After a few months he ran away, and set out on a worldwide journey. He walked through all of southern Europe until he reached Turkey. Returning to Vienna, he joined the police. He became a fiery National Socialist and considered Hitler a god. He was one of the first Austrian policemen to join the party. Still in the time of Dollfuss, he became a secret member of the SS. After the annexation of Austria he changed to an irreconcilable enemy of Hitler—the first to join—the first to turn away. His attitude towards the Jewish population was relatively sympathetic. With sincere compassion, he helped as much as he could during each Aktion. He did this cleverly so as not to arouse suspicion among his colleagues. "Screaming is the best mask for my attitude," he would say, and everyone knew about it. Jews, after recognizing his true character, confided in him. He aided many to escape—to carry out luggage. Occasionally he would escort a Jew as a prisoner, thus helping him to cross the frontier. During the hard times he supplied Jews with bread and fats, personally bringing food to the post. Of course his efforts were recompensed, although this was not necessarily true in all cases. However, he never did anything to hurt anyone. After the last deportation, many Jews hid in the ghetto. Some of their hiding places were known to Bousko. Quite a number of Jews owed their lives to him. Many Poles received his aid as well.

In July 1944, when the Germans were retreating quickly in the East, the danger of being drafted to the front threatened Bousko. In order to avoid this, he injected himself intramuscularly with Propidon, causing artificially large abcesses. He became feverish, forcing the medical commission to move him into the hospital—dragging it out in this manner for several weeks. When he realized that he could not "ride the same horse" any longer, he vanished. Disguised, he escaped into the environs of Kalwaria, and hiding there he had—it was rumored—a Polish girlfriend, two Jewish children under his care, and a sizable valise containing valuables he received in payment for favors while serving in the ghetto.

The disappearance of Bousko could not be kept secret for long. The chief of the German police in Podgorze started the search because in those days German policemen were frequently taken hostage by the Polish partisans.

Bousko learned about this and decided to use it to his advantage. He wrote to his commander, claiming to be in the hands of the partisans, but he did not know where; even if he knew, he could not tell. His life depended on whether the Poles from the last list of the condemned would be executed. This letter marked the beginning of his undoing. An intensive search began and he was soon caught, at the point of crossing the frontier. He was transferred to Cracow and jailed in the Montelupich prison. A few weeks later he was moved to Danzig where he unsuccessfully feigned insanity. He was sentenced to death by a court-martial and executed on October 18, 1944.

After the desertion of Bousko was discovered, the Germans remained agitated for the longest time. They just couldn't forgive the fact that they were duped into having so much confidence in him and were so deceived. Now they suspected him of everything. Each Jewish escape from the ghetto was credited to him. They blamed him for every unsuccessful German Aktion, claiming that Bousko betrayed the official secrets to the Jews. The subordinates of Bousko were: two Viennese—Essel, a shoemaker by trade, a well-meaning man; Breczko, a degenerate homosexual; Vita, Volksdeutsch from Silesia, who was later arrested by the Germans for armed robbery; and Schubert, a cunning man, who used to bring secret newspapers. All of them generally behaved rather decently.

The ghetto was still surrounded by Sonderdienst. I came back to the pharmacy, this time in the company of a blue policeman. We saw the German police guards marching in fours with rifles at the ready. Now and then, they would shoot at windows when they saw someone looking out.

Meanwhile, in the ghetto, a directive of the German authorities was issued regarding a new registration procedure for the Kennkarten, regardless of whether they were previously stamped by the SS. Everyone was ordered to report Saturday, June 6, 1942, in the building on Jozefinska Street with work papers and identity passes in order to obtain the so-called Blauschein. From early morning, people waited anxiously and nervously for the result of the registration. A committee of the Gestapo issued or refused the Blauschein. Neither professional qualifications nor work assignments influenced the decision to grant the cards. Those who did not receive them were immediately detained, and after a while, were transferred, together with others, to the courtyard of "Optima" on Wegierska Street. No one was permitted to take anything along. Among the Gestapo were OD men mingling and maintaining order. Förster, Spira, Pacanower, Wertal, Susser—all in the service of the Gestapo—acted to intervene. These intercessions, accompanied by bribes of money, gifts of gold, and costly jewelry, were usually successful.

German workshop managers also intervened on behalf of their employees, some of whom were highly qualified technically. These intercessions, however, were less successful because they lacked "tangible" wherewithall.

A new regulation was put into effect. It warned that anyone who was caught without a Blauschein after the posted time would be shot. Any regulation, directive, or order issued by German authorities always contained a death threat. It therefore made no real impact; on the contrary, it provoked jokes. Each natural death was considered, at the time, to be a comparatively happy circumstance.

The courtyard of Optima was filling with deportees. Ironically, the weather was beautiful. The sun was scorching. The air was humid and sticky—particularly difficult for old people and the sick. Without water, often without a piece of bread, the Jews sat under the oppressive heat of the broiling sun, awaiting their fate. Despite two previous deportations, despite the fact that they had witnessed all these scenes previously, they would not admit to themselves that they feared what was in store for them. This was exemplified by the kind of requests directed to their close relatives through the OD men. They asked for warm clothing, money, soap, and other essentials. The interventions by the Judenrat, OD, and workshop managers continued.

At any given moment someone would rush into the pharmacy and ask for help for relatives or friends awaiting departure in the Optima courtyard. The ladies working in the pharmacy were busy dispensing medications, food, and cigarettes. The admirable Dr. D. Schlang and his wife Dora were extremely helpful during this period.

Again, we were successful in obtaining several Blauschein from Kunde—everything depended on happy coincidence or accident. Nothing could be foreseen or planned. Thanks to these blue pieces of paper, several of our acquaintances returned to the ghetto, and at night we drank to the miraculous rescue that allowed us to spend a few joyful hours.

Occasionally someone left the courtyard and in his place OD men would bring replacements from the building in which the committee officiated. The terrible Saturday night passed. The members of the Sonderdienst searched the people waiting in the Optima courtyard. They seized everything of value. At seven o'clock Sunday morning they brought new groups of people. I saw venerable women, old men barely able to move their feet, very sick men who were pulled out of the hospitals, invalids who had to be led by hand—all of them headed for torment.

Some people had been sitting in the square for almost two days without water or food, and in blistering heat.

The 8th of June arrived. The deportation began: people arose, calls were heard, as well as shouts of the German guards. The gate of the Optima courtyard was opened. The first deportees left the courtyard and huddled in groups surrounded by strong Sonderdienst guards. The rifles in the hands of the Germans were in a ready position to shoot. The procession moved through Limanowska and Wielicka Streets to the railroad station in Prokocim where these unfortunates were loaded into the waiting train. Many cars already contained deportees from Miechowa, Jedrzejow, and Slomnik. From this Cracow transport a handful of people were saved. They were separated by the Gestapo and transferred to "Julag," the labor camp in Plaszow.

During the deportations, the hospitals were also emptied. It was therefore obvious that during each Aktion those who were strong enough or were able, would leave the hospital, hiding in strange houses, waiting until the trouble was over to return to the hospital.

Unfortunately, no one knew how, the Germans discovered that the hospital was full again. They ordered three doctors, Fischer, Bornstein, and Engelstein, to make a selection among the sick to reduce their number to a bare minimum. This order was humanely impossible to obey. Who could decide which patient would live or which one would die, who would take this awesome responsibility, what would be the decisive criteria? The dignity, fairness, and sacrifice of Dr. Bornstein should be pointed out, because one of the patients who was unable to move was his mother. He did not try to save her at the expense of another life.

A bold conception of Dr. Julian Aleksandrowicz's wife Maryla, and its audacious execution by Julek was admired by all who knew the background of the problem. Aleksandrowicz deceived the Germans, leading a few of the invalids and people out on stretchers and joining them to a long line of people who were preparing to leave the ghetto. He reported to the Germans that their order was carried out, and pointed to the group of patients, invalids and people on stretchers; the Germans believed that in this group were all of the patients taken out of the hospital. As soon as the Germans withdrew, the patients evaporated like steam, leaving the lines to hide in private homes or in various corners of basements or attics, there to wait out the deportation.

In the three stages of the first June deportation from the ghetto 7,000 people were expelled. It was learned later that all the transports were routed to the extermination camp in Belzec.

The fate of the deportees became the main topic of conversation in the ghetto. The relatives left behind tried to discover something definite about their dear ones in every possible way. All kinds of rumors were circulated. The most improbable gossip was attributed to "unimpeachable" sources. The source of this news was always the Germans, the so-called decent ones, who purportedly betrayed the secrets of the German authorities. This was a well-known ploy to divert vigilance and to raise some hope that the deportees were alive, to avoid causing extreme despair and to abort any attempt at revolt.

Making the rounds was the news that the deportees were being sent to the Ukraine and that they were working on farms there. Some German railroaders related that they observed a tremendous number of barracks, and Jews there from all over Europe. They were doing well, they worked hard, but they had all the essentials they needed for living, including food and clothing. They were, of course, well guarded—by barbed wire—no one could get close there—they were not permitted to write letters so no news was available. Many requests flooded the narrators of these stories. They were asked to go there, to take news from here and to return with replies. The Germans naturally refused, to begin with—they could not do it then, perhaps later—all this designed to present utmost difficulties and to raise the price. People disregarded the cost; they paid whatever was demanded, just to maintain a glimmer of hope. No encouragement, no certainty, ever reached the ghetto. The Germans took their money, disappeared like vapor, and the people waited and believed.

I knew a Pole, Tataruch by name, who was married to a Jew in the ghetto who was sent into the unknown. He looked everywhere trying to find her —even in Ukraine—but found no trace of barracks of Jews working there. One could not understand why entire trains of deportees vanished so mysteriously. No one could even guess where the transports were sent. After several months news began to trickle into the ghetto; for the first time names were mentioned: Belzec, Majdanek, Treblinka, death camps with tall smoking crematory chimneys.

In spite of everything, the thought of mass murders, gas chambers, and crematoria was not yet conceivable. More often, news brought stories of cruelties during the loading of people into the railroad cars, about mysterious stations without a name, about dead-end runs of trains, crowded with people who waited without food and water for days on end, only to disappear into the dense forests, enclosed by barbed wire from behind which no voices were ever heard. There were conjectures that the deportees disappeared into secret factories to produce new weapons that the Germans were assembling, but in no case was there any talk about these people going to their death.

Then, one beautiful sunny day, news spread with lightning speed by word of mouth about a man from the transport whose destination was Belzec, who saved himself and returned to the ghetto. Who was this hero? How could he, one of so many thousands, save himself? What was he saying? What about the rest of the deportees? What fate awaited them? Questions without end . . . This brave man was the dentist Bachner. He ran from the transport. Risking everything on one slim chance, he entered the nearest latrine and jumped into the pit. Immersed to his chest in human excrement, he remained there for several days. When the last of the deportees were gone and stillness returned, he escaped at night from this terrible hideout and slowly wandered in the direction of Cracow until he reached the ghetto, the place from where, just a short while ago, he had moved into the unknown.

Only from him, the dentist Bachner, the refugee from the extermination transport, did the ghetto learn that it was true, that there existed camps in which the Germans murdered incoming prisoners by gas and cremation. The nightmarish stories Bachner told were incomprehensible to the human mind. Was it possible that in the twentieth century any nation could sink so low, a people who were world-renowned for their great humanists, their foremost thinkers and philosophers?

Today, when we quietly consider the method used to execute these victims of the three June deportations, we are able to expose the well-planned perfidy the Germans used to deceive and rob these people not only of their lives but also of their personal possessions; we see the cleverly conceived directives to inflict their indignities with greater ease.

The first order regarding deportation sounded innocent enough. Because they felt it was needed to ease the overcrowding in the ghetto to provide adequate living conditions for the remaining inhabitants, and to prevent the danger of epidemics, the authorities were compelled to resettle part of the Jewish population. Everyone could take along all they could carry.

People took immense quantities of luggage, selecting only the most valuable items. They assumed that the same fate awaited them as did the previous evacuees who were transported to the vicinity of Lublin and released there. Or perhaps, they thought, they would be transferred to another ghetto. On the first transport they appeared with practically all of their luggage. Their belongings were taken away from them at the Plaszow railroad station but no personal search was instituted. This would probably take place at the destination point. The purpose of it all was to convince those in the succeeding transport that small items could be carried and it was advisable to give up the larger ones. The Germans were convinced that in such cases everybody would carry small valuable pieces, such as jewels, gold, and money. In the second deportation, the Germans used a different method: they made the personal search on the spot, seizing whatever was possible. What they did not find here, their colleagues would discover at the point of destination. Larger bundles and luggage were generally appropriated at Plac Zgody, and what was left in the houses was taken by the workmen brought in by Baudienst.

During the third deportation, people without the blue cards were detained then and there; they were not permitted to take anything from their apartments, which were sealed by the OD.

On the 10th of June, the German guards left the ghetto. The Jews, emotionally exhausted, were able to breathe easier. After a week-long atmosphere of fear, uncertainty about what the next day would bring, the Jews, nervously spent, started to return at least superficially to normal equilibrium, although there were frequent mental breakdowns. During the three deportations a considerable number of suicides occurred, mostly by the use of cyanide or gas. At first, getting a supply of the poison was a difficult task. Later, a source was found: the lamp factory of Wachs on Lwowska Street used cyanide in the manufacture of their products. There, people were able to obtain this poison, which was coveted as a priceless treasure. Entire families always carried it with them in small bottles just—as the saying goes—in case.

In the first weeks of deportation, many people looked for ways to get out of the ghetto. In fact, quite a number of them were successful. The family of Dr. Oberlander, Mgr. Jutkiewicz, with his mother and sister, Mrs. Feliks, wife of a well-known Cracow physician, Dr. Jozef Feliks, with her daughter left the apartment house in which the pharmacy was located. The escape from the ghetto and the trip to Warsaw were organized and facilitated for these people by the mysterious and controversial Förster. Virtually all of those listed perished during the Warsaw Uprising or sometimes earlier. For instance, Nathan Oberlander died as a result of a bombing. His wife buried him in the courtyard of their apartment house. She survived the occupation and returned to Cracow, where we met frequently.

Except for extreme pessimists, there was no dearth of those in the ghetto who observed the occurrences uncritically, people who could not accurately evaluate the events that occurred and who still believed the Germans. They insisted, with fanatic stubbornness, in their belief that the deportations were the last act in the Jewish tragedy. These were chiefly the people who worked on the German projects where the Germans spread their lies, and the Jews represented them in the ghetto as incontrovertible truth. However, most of the inhabitants no longer trusted this assurance.

A few days after the June deportation, an announcement appeared regarding the reduction of the ghetto's boundaries. The following streets were excluded from the area: Rekawka, part of Krakus and Wegierska Streets, all of Czarniecka Street, including the court and prison located there, and the right side of Limanowska Street (starting from Podgorze's main square). The Judenrat housing office, headed by the lawyer Dr. Jakub Wasserlauf, was assigned the task of relocating the remaining people. The walls, no longer necessary, were partially demolished and posts connected with barbed wire were installed. The ghetto's appearance changed somehow: it became more visible from the "Aryan" side. Immediately after the publication of the announcement, a new movement of people and their belongings took place. It was reminiscent of the time of the formation of the ghetto, but now it proceeded at a faster pace, more nervously and with greater anxiety. From morning until late at night, people scurried, carrying their possessions on their shoulders, hauling bundles of linen, valises, trunks, baskets, bearing individual pieces of furniture and the priceless treasures of coal and firewood. Very few could afford transportation by carts and wagons; this was very expensive. For several days the traffic was impossible. The ghetto lived on its frazzled nerves, completely exhausted both mentally and physically.

The deportation was carried out on the date prescribed by the authorities. Life started to return to normal, but only outwardly. Time was passing, healing the wounds and partially deadening the painful emptiness caused by the disruption and destruction of families. The spark of life, however, continued to glow. People did not surrender; they started to reorganize. The stores, which were closed on the streets cut off from the ghetto, reopened in new locations. The shops of the deported owners fell in many cases into the hands of new proprietors. But the peace which existed before did not return. Apprehension increased the vigilance. Even the slightest suspicious detail evoked distrust; the most innocent sounding regulation of any authority caused unending comments, suppositions, and predictions. Life became more and more difficult, the freedom of the individual was sharply curtailed, the rules governing trips to the city became more stringent, and the obtaining of passes become more difficult. The Arbeitsamt officiated with broad powers: new files, new work assignments, new controls of the employees. Hospitals were full. Those exhausted by overwork, the malnourished, and those who were mistreated physically and morally increased in number. It was not surprising, therefore, that diseases and suicides were rampant.

There were four hospitals in the ghetto: The Central Hospital, transferred there from Skawinska Street to the Jewish quarter at the corner of Jozefinska and Wegierska Streets, its director was Dr. Nussenfeld, a renowned surgeon in Cracow; the Hospital for Infectious Diseases on Rekawka Street, expertly administered by Dr. A. Biberstein, after the ghetto was contracted, cutting off Rekawka Street, this hospital was transferred to a little side-street off Plac Zgody; the small hospital on Limanowska Street, which specialized in geriatrics, it was headed by a magnificent man, Dr. Kranz, who perished together with the patients during the June 1942 deportation; the Hospital for Convalescent Care, supervised by two great humanitarians, men of great knowledge and deep dedication: Dr. Julian Aleksandrowicz and Dr. Bernstein.

During all the deportations and bloody Aktions, these hospitals played an important role in sheltering people by certifying them as severely ill. Endangered people who came seeking help received false diagnoses and cleverly prepared places of concealment.

I visited all of the hospitals in the ghetto area, I went to almost every old age home, and I was amazed at the ingenuity and selflessness of the hospitals' directors and staffs. I saw in what high esteem the patients regarded Dr. Aleksandrowicz; I heard expressions of gratitude for Dr. Kranz and his able assistant, Mrs. Gutman. At the principal hospital on Jozefinska Street, after its transfer from Skawinska Street, I was pleasantly surprised at how, in the newly painted and renovated building, all of the regular departments of a conventional hospital were installed, although the Germans allowed little enough to be transferred. The operating room was quite busy. Operation after operation was performed all day long. Apart from the ghetto doctors (Nussenfeld, Ferdinand Lewkowicz, and Blau), surgeons from the city were also called in on difficult cases in the early days of the ghetto, provided with special passes. Members of the faculty, like Professors Jan Glatzel and J. Zubrzycki, often operated. Professors Tadeusz Tempka, Aleksander Oszacki, and Dr. Stanislaw Lapinski were available for medical consultations. The heads of the Department of Internal Medicine were Drs. Blassberg and Glassner; the Neurological Department head was Dr. Bornstein; Gynecology, Dr. J. Lachs and a woman, Dr. R. Feniger; Urology, Dr. R. Lachs; Ophthalmology, Drs. A. Mrowski and Michal Schel; Laryngology, Drs. Feliks Grunbaum and Edward Mahauf; Dermatology, Drs. Rosenzweig and Henryk Engelstein; Radiology was directed by Drs. Stefan Schwarz and Czeslaw Blunbaum. The chief of the Hospital for Infectious Diseases was Dr. A. Biberstein, for whom the patients had the highest admiration. The head of the Department of Health and the liaison with the German authorities was Dr. Haber.

Other than these officials, virtually all of the other doctors worked in the hospitals for no fees.

The focal point after each deportation was the pharmacy. It was common knowledge that those who escaped headed there; others waited as well; there too appeared those in the circle of friends whom fate saved from death. Each one told how he ran, where he hid, and how he was rescued. Joy and despair—some rejoiced at being alive; others were grief-stricken at the loss of their loved ones. Twinges of conscience overcame all; they could not forgive themselves for past acts that brought pain to those close to them; they tried to convince themselves that their misdeeds were not the result of ill will but were momentary misunderstandings caused by the anxieties of life and the constant fear of death. The anguish deepened. The macabre mood seemed to make people whisper; tears inhibited the raising of voices. One imagined that they were hearing the clicking of train wheels over the rails, leading nowhere. And so we were mired in the silent despair of our friends. The door of the pharmacy will never again be opened by the hands of such acquaintances, friends and frequent guests as Doctors Stanislaw Eibenschutz, Dora Haber, Maurycy Haber, and Dora Silberger. They are gone forever.

The task of the Judenrat was very difficult. I have already mentioned Commissioner Gutter. I also got better acquainted with Counselor Streimer, a man of about 55 years, dangerously astute, well-educated, who spoke several languages. I talked with him several times about general subjects. I had been forewarned by Schor to be extremely cautious with this man because his exact relationship with the Germans was not quite clear. I therefore tried to lead the conversation in an effort to ascertain what truth, if any, occasioned the suspicions. The views he expressed were always well-reasoned. It was obvious that his thoughts on many current topics were well-organized beforehand. He weighed each word, cleverly adopting an economy of expression. I did not find out anything for a certainty; each answer, particularly when a political question was involved, was ambiguous enough to present two alternatives. Dr. Streimer was a man who was unusually sure of himself, bragging about his knowledge of the German psyche and his capability of successfully dealing with it. He was a very stubborn, unyielding man, never smiling, of somber mien—a rather unpleasant individual. He was shot by the Germans in the Plaszow camp. Who he really was and what role he played in the ghetto was a secret he took to his grave.

One of the hardest working members of the Judenrat, from the very beginning, was Mgr. Leon Salpeter, my older professional colleague, a man of lofty ideals, always levelheaded and pleasant. When I repeatedly asked him why he did not escape from the ghetto, he would explain that even if he had the opportunity and could do so, he never would. He would remain with the people to the end. What he decided to do, he achieved. He stayed, endured, and survived until the Germans were defeated. Immediately after the war, he participated in the Zionist Congress in London as one of the delegates representing the Polish Jews. He emigrated to Israel, where he opened his own pharmacy in Jaffa. During my stay in that country, I was a frequent guest in the house of Mr. and Mrs. Salpeter. The kindly Mrs. Elizabeth, wife of Leon, tried to make my stay as pleasant as possible. In 1967, we were all together in Cologne at the court proceedings against Kunde, who did not live to hear his sentence. He died of cancer soon after. Poor Salpeter passed away after major surgery in 1968.

Counselor-Director Salmonowicz, about 57 years old, calm and wise, would help everyone with good advice; a man of unquestionable decency, he helped wherever and whenever he could. He knew how to talk with the Germans . . . Because of his intervention, several people were saved from the June deportation.

The work in the Judenrat was very hateful for conscientious people. It was easy to carry out orders against one's will, to circumvent the law, to play for delays, to quietly and tactfully convince the multitude of people that the Judenrat did not issue any orders but, under duress, merely obeyed the Germans' demands. Many people looked with a jaundiced eye at the Judenrat activities in the ghetto, although they could not reproach its members—except, of course, in a few cases—with any concrete evidence. After the war I repeatedly heard the opinion expressed that those who held the so-called "higher positions" should have resigned. Forgotten was the fact that resignation from such a position was tantamount to signing one's death warrant, including the family. After all, someone had to occupy those positions. Was it not better that the majority of the Judenrat were fair people—that in their places there might have been appointed characters in the service of the Germans, as it sometimes happened? To be a hero, to sacrifice your life for an ideal, is undoubtedly noble, but this had to be inbred. Not everyone is born a genius, and not everyone can be a hero. It was always thus, and it will always remain that way. Besides, it was significant to me that the invectives and epithets hurled at the members of the Judenrat were heard only after the war, when the charged atmosphere and the harrowing circumstances were quickly forgotten. Most of the reproaches were voiced by those who lived through the occupation far from Poland and did not suffer through the deportations or the climate of terror prevalent in such situations. They simply did not really know the true character of the Germans and the occupation from personal experience. I am unalterably convinced that were it not for the fact that there were so many decent and honorable members in the Judenrat, the fate of the ghetto dwellers might have been much worse.

Many people who lived through the war outside of Poland did not realize what surviving in the ghetto entailed. In 1965, when I was in America, I met a dear friend from the Gymnasium, where we had shared the same bench. On the very first day we met—my friend was a Jew—the conversation turned to my memories of the Cracow ghetto.

"Tadeusz," he said, "I read your little book—I even liked it—but you must have exaggerated your description of the murders and mistreatment the Germans inflicted on the Jews. It doesn't matter that you were carried away by your fantasy—the Germans had it coming to them, both of us knew the truth."

"Henryk," I said to him, "where did you live during that time, in what world, that you don't believe me? I was there, of course, throughout the period of the ghetto's existence, I lived with those people—I was an eyewitness, together with the ladies employed in my pharmacy, of everything that went on in Plac Zgody during the deportations, and not only there but all over, and you can talk about exaggerations?" No reasoning helped. After a while, with a slight smile, he patted me on the shoulder and said, "Let's leave these sad things alone—let us drink to our happier past—to today—and to tomorrow."

To this day I remember that conversation, and I ask myself, how many people are there in the world who also think that way?

The attitude of the German authorities was doubtless worse toward the Judenrat than toward the OD. The Judenrat definitely delivered far less material benefits, which, after all, was what the Germans were most interested in. There was no question about the lack of confidence the Gestapo had in the Judenrat, while on the whole there was some confidence in the OD, especially in certain individuals who were blindly loyal. Spira of the OD knew the German attitude toward the Judenrat well. He stressed his higher influence on every occasion, at first waging a kind of quiet war against the Judenrat and its president, Rosenzweig, and later against Commissioner Gutter. From each skirmish Spira would emerge victorious. Both of them resembled each other physically: spare and emaciated. Both of them also had similar character traits: unusually nervous, impetuous, pathological, hubristic, extremely erotic sensitivity, seeking easy conquests. Gutter surpassed Spira intellectually and possessed superior rhetorical talents, was more polished in his behavior toward those who imposed on him. The Gestapo reinforced Spira's sense of power and fueled the fire of his megalomania. Thus Spira, along with several of his closest cronies, enjoyed privileges not available to any other Jew. He had the freedom to leave the ghetto, to walk about without an armband, to use a droshky, to enter Gestapo headquarters at will. He knew nearly all of the Gestapo men and they knew him. He had a talent for presenting appropriate gifts, even for the smallest favors. Spira's admiration for his immediate superior, Kunde, knew no bounds. Not infrequently one could hear Spira brag: "Nobody else but Spira will survive the war; everybody else will perish, but Spira will live." And he was partially correct. People live and die in the normal course of events and the names of the most upright are consigned to oblivion. Spira's name will not be erased from human memory. Every chronicle, every memoir, any mention of the Cracow ghetto will remind posterity of Symche Spira, formerly a glazier—in the ghetto, the head of the OD, lord of life and death of tens of thousands of Jews.

Days and nights passed with constant worry and problems. The paucity of living space became increasingly acute. In the second half of November 1942, the Germans issued a directive concerning a new contraction of the ghetto: the inhabitants of the so-called "Ukraina," which were the streets to the left of Lwowska, had to vacate within one day and move to what was left of the ghetto. Despair gripped the people. The relocation commenced; furniture was left behind; only the most essential items were taken. But, wonder of wonders, for the first time in the history of the ghetto, a revocation of this directive was accomplished. The Jews carried their belongings back to their abandoned apartments. What joy! There was a great deal of talk about this, but soon terrible disappointment awaited the inhabitants.

I remember a typical incident that occurred in that period. It was just a few months after the June deportation, while everyone could still remember the cruel and bestial treatment the Germans had unleashed on the defenseless population.

One morning, a long column of German cars passed through Plac Zgody toward Limanowska Street—a long parade of cars rolling east. One of the cars hit a young Jewish boy running across the street. The car stopped and behind it so did the whole line of German cars. Someone lifted the boy and carried him to the hospital. The German police arrived. At their headquarters on Franciszkanska Street, they had been informed of the accident by telephone by the local OD. Investigations began, the policemen measured the distances, asked about the speed of the offending car, then finally wrote their report. After a delay of almost an hour, the cars started moving again. I could not understand it, with the memory still vivid of so many killed, what a senseless adherence to regulations, what an extraordinary example of bureaucracy! The boy, only slightly bruised, recovered very quickly; he regained his health only to lose his life in the first Aktion where mass murders were already beyond the control of law.

Days were all alike because they were uniformly tiring, uniformly fraught with uncertainty. People returned to the ghetto daily from various work assignments with all kinds of news and gossip pertaining to the ghetto's fate. Rumors spread again about a new deportation, later about the complete liquidation of the ghetto, about Plaszow, and a closed camp outside the ghetto area. The Germans categorically denied this, and it made the people most anxious. It was everyone's opinion that the situation was quite different from the version of the SS and the Gestapo. Bringing order and completing the files in the Arbeitsamt caused considerable worry. Something ominous was imminent.

The mood in the ghetto worsened with each passing day. The 27th of October 1942, arrived. Everyone knew that a deportation would take place on the following day. Spira left the ghetto by droshky several times. He returned upset and very nervous, but remained silent and did not tell even his closest associates the substance of his talks with the Gestapo authorities. New Gestapo men appeared in the ghetto streets and all of them went to the building where the Jewish police were located and where the Germans who were in direct contact with the affairs of the ghetto had separate offices.

The specialists for Jewish matters who belonged to the Sicherheitspolizei were: SS Obersturmführer Becher, SS Oberscharführer Siebert, Untersturmführer Brand. These officials appeared in the ghetto from time to time. SS Sturmscharführer Kriminalsekretär Wilhelm Kunde, Olde, and SS Obersturmführer Hermann Heinrich were permanently stationed there.

The specialists for Jewish affairs on behalf of the Gestapo were: SS Obersturmführer Theodor Heinermayer, Specialists SIPO Korner and Paul Mallotke. Representing the SS U. Polizei were: SS Oberführer Scherner, Sturmbannführer Hasse, SS Unterscharführer Horst Pilarzik, SS Rottenführer Wiktor Ritschek, and SS Rottenführer Zugsberger.

Several times that day, Gutter went to Oleanders where the main office of SS U. Polizei was located; there he spoke with Oberführer SS U. Polizei Scherner, the highest authority for Jewish affairs in the Cracow district.

The results of the decisive conference were negative; the purported efforts of Gutter to move the deportation date came to naught.

Under the threat of losing his life, Gutter was forbidden to mention the Aktion, which was to take place the next day. He returned; the secret could not be kept. In a few minutes, the entire ghetto knew what to expect on the following day. People seriously prepared for the expected Aktion. Everyone knew full well from past experiences that whoever was not deported, even though lacking the "stamp" but able to remain in hiding for some time, could later obtain the stamp and no one would worry too much about its authenticity. Experience taught us that one did not have to take the regulations of the German authorities too seriously because they always threatened the death penalty. People became fatalists and entrusted their destiny to fate. The lot of the deportees was evident to some and they sabotaged the orders of the authorities. If they were successful—fine; if not—they would die; sooner or later this would happen. Of the two options, they preferred to hide.

Feverishly, people began to prepare hiding places. Those who had the physical capacity with strong nerves to endure uncomfortable positions for many hours, amid the shouts and screams of the Germans surrounding them, would virtually disappear from the ghetto, concealed in the most ingeniously contrived hideouts. They found these places in basements, attics, and within apartments. I remember how one of my acquaintances hid her parents in the foyer, in a pantry from which she removed the shelves and covered the opening with a wooden panel on which were coat hooks and a mirror as seen in modern apartments. She nailed the panel tightly against the wall. The Germans who searched the apartment thoroughly during the course of an Aktion never suspected that anyone could be concealed behind the coat hooks.

Many fled Cracow to reach close friends and to stay with them for a few days. When the Aktion was over, they returned to the ghetto. I met several such persons in the city and I talked with them. In the case of Dr. Nattel's wife, I was fortunate to find a room for her on Mikolajska Street, where she hid during the Aktion that ended after one day.

At about five in the afternoon, I returned to the ghetto. A mood of depression was pervasive; nervous people gathered in groups in the street, discussing what lay in store for them. Nobody doubted that there would be a deportation on the next day. Anxiety became more intense as the hours passed; the women were terrified about the fate of their children and walked about aimlessly as if demented. The pharmacy was full—we sold tranquilizers almost exclusively—virtually no one brought in a prescription. Who would think of going to a doctor, when tomorrow one's very survival was in doubt. At approximately eight o'clock in the evening, the inhabitants learned from those returning home from work and from the blue police that a large, fully armed platoon of the Sonderdienst was marching through the streets of Cracow toward Podgorze. The pharmacy was full of acquaintances. Married couples and others with children asked what could be done. Doctors (supposedly immune) and single persons were calm.

At about nine that night, a platoon of Sonderdienst surrounded the ghetto with armed soldiers. There was no longer any possibility of escape. We spent a long, sleepless, and tiring night. No one knew what criteria the Germans would use for segregation this time. Food was supplied to the prepared hideouts. In the pharmacy, from time to time, someone would request Luminal, a sleeping drug, in children's dosages. What for? It was administered to small children, and even babies, so that they would not betray the hiding places by crying. That very day, in the late evening, a directive was transmitted, mostly orally by the Judenrat, ordering all workers to line up on the next day, October 28, in the early morning in front of the Jewish community places. The night of October 27 was awful. In the pharmacy from night until dawn many people, extremely anxious, in a macabre mood, came in to consult with those present, then left only to appear again in a few hours. Before dawn the pharmacy was emptied out. I was left alone. I realized full well that my coworkers would not be able to reach the pharmacy that day. Reinforced police posts did not permit anyone to enter without special permission from the Gestapo.

October 28—a beautiful, almost springlike day, the cloudless sky reminded one of the time of the June deportation. People congregated at the exit gate at Wegierska Street in front of the community building. Many, on their way to work, brought their small children with them; they hoped that they would be able to take them along and, on occasion, the German managers would intercede for them with the police authorities.

At six o'clock in the morning, cars arrived carrying the dignitaries of the SS and the Gestapo. SS Sturmbahnführer Haase, in whose hands was the control of the Aktion, was present. He was a man of about 40 years of age, but looked very much older. Tall, lean, gray hair, with steely penetrating eyes, he never smiled; he was married and father of four children, the youngest was two years old. Haase was supposed to direct the October deportation personally.

Apart from the SS, Gestapo, officials of the Arbeitsamt, and "guests" from the district, the managers of various German shops employing Jews tried to release experienced specialists who were destined for deportation. Occasionally there were cases of sincere sympathy and willingness to help individual Jews, as I could judge from the stories of those directly concerned. Usually, each of the Germans acted in his own interests because the loss of workers and first-class specialists could cause the liquidation of the shop, resulting in consignment of the manager to the front. Each was interested, therefore, in protecting his Jews from deportation.

The guards prepared to march away from Wegierska Street. The Gestapo and SS carried out the selection without any particular directives. The age, physical stature, and general appearance decided whether the Gestapo would direct the worker to the exit gate or allow him to remain in the ghetto. In rare cases were the shop managers able to change the decision of the Gestapo. Loud shouts—names of people who would stay in the ghetto—were called out to exclude certain persons from some groups. All this happened accompanied by the terrifying shouts of the Germans. Whips lashed out aimlessly at the crowd. Gutter, the officials of the Judenrat, and Spira with his staff, ran from one German to another. Only a few were able to smuggle out a child, taking advantage of the inattention and confusion of the Gestapo, but as a rule, the children were separated from their parents.

The workers left the ghetto. Strong units of the Sonderdienst entered, fully armed, in two columns, and halted at Plac Zgody. They stacked their rifles. From Jozefinska Street and from the direction of Lwowska Street one could hear the thumping cadence of the hobnailed boots of the German police units. Armed spies, collaborators from Lithuania and Latvia who served in the German units and distinguished themselves with displays of unusual cruelty and sadism, also entered the ghetto. They were used in the Aktions for the liquidation of the ghetto.

I was all alone in the pharmacy. None of the personnel was allowed to enter that day. I did not open the pharmacy, but displayed a card asking people to ring the bell in case of need. I stayed in my room, one meter away from the window so as not to be seen by the Germans out in front. They ordered all the ghetto inhabitants, without exception, to leave their houses by ten o'clock in the morning to report at Jozefinska Street and to line up on the block between the community and OD buildings. Anyone who remained at home after ten o'clock would be shot immediately.

Throngs of people left their apartments, which they were not allowed to lock. Jozefinska Street filled rapidly. The SS and Gestapo casually glanced at the papers—with a wave of the hand, they sentenced some to deportation, others were permitted to remain. Again, they did not make their decisions using any particular standards. Luck, caprice, or accident were responsible for their choices. Doctors and members of the Judenrat wore special armbands which were supposed to protect them from deportation and give them freedom of movement. They used this privilege only in exceptional cases. The physicians were ordered to congregate in the hospital. It appeared that the armbands did not help. I witnessed the Germans, who for some reason did not like someone, select him for deportation in spite of the armband. I saw how Mgr. of Pharmacy Immergluck and his wife were pushed into the transport even though they belonged to the sanitary commission. No explanation or presentation of papers helped. Germans calmly took their documents and, without reading them, tore them up. I saw a German kick the physician Dr. Sigmund Leinkram toward the deportees.

More and more people, pushed with rifle butts and beaten, accompanied by seemingly unceasing shouts from the SS men, ran to the square. Haase wanted to bring all of the Jews out of concealment from their ingeniously prepared and camouflaged hiding places. He stepped out on a platform at the convergence of several apartment houses and he raised his arm. Deadly stillness. "Alle Manner und Frauen gehen ruhig nach hause" (All men and women, go home quietly), he said. The quiet was broken by the shouts of joy of the hundreds of people who heard these words. Their elation did not last very long. Again Haase raised his hand, the dreadful stillness, and the German words: "Um ihre notwendigste Sachen mitzunehmen. Ghetto ist Judenrein!" (In order to take the most necessary things. The ghetto is free of Jews!) Now everything was clear. The news spread like wildfire through the entire ghetto, stealthily pervading each house, each room, and reaching even the best concealed hideouts. Many people were taken in by the lie, and left their hiding places, only to suffer the same fate of the others.

Among them were the children of the Weintraub family, well-known in the ghetto. The despairing parents had hidden the children in the furniture, which was then placed on the wagons bound for Plaszow, where a camp was being hastily erected. The children were concealed in one of the barracks which was under construction. Unfortunately they did not make use of their new hiding place for long. Because of the betrayal by mean people, the information about the hidden ones reached the Germans very quickly and the children were shot moments later. This was not an isolated case. There was a Mrs. Chilowicz, an informer, whose task it was to find out where there were children hidden in the camp and to report their whereabouts to the Germans. Very often, as a result of this treachery, not only were the children shot, but also their parents.

The first shots were heard; the first victims of the October deportation were falling in the courtyards, halls, and sidewalks. There were the bloodied wounded, there were bodies. Hitler's executioners watched the awful agony of the murdered. A wall of silence enveloped both sides. The crowd in the square grew. The standees were ordered to sit. Standing was forbidden; even the need to perform biological functions was not allowed. The crowds were unbelievable. There was no water. This time there were no doctors in the square, no one could bring any help, and the heat was insufferable. These Dantesque scenes would remain forever in the memory of people like me who saw and lived through them.

What was happening to those who went to work could easily be imagined. Without any idea of what was happening in the ghetto, they consoled themselves with the assurances of the Germans that their families would be protected. The working people were mostly men; the deportees were their wives, parents, and children, who left without any hope of saying good-bye to their dear ones. The deportees were also old people taken from nursing homes, from shelters, patients from hospitals, where the rule was that no one was allowed to leave his bed.

At about twelve o'clock noon, SS men invaded the main hospital at Jozefinska Street and shot the patients who were not able to run away. The Germans beat anyone in the hall, expelled the hospital personnel, didn't even have any respect for a woman who was giving birth. They ordered her thrown on a flat truck which was parked in front of the hospital, prepared for patients whom they did not manage to kill on the spot. The command was fulfilled. Nearly a score of physicians lost their lives in this Aktion.

In the square, the officers of SS and the Gestapo of various ranks were milling around. Almost everyone had some sort of truncheon or a club in his hand, and there was no lack of those armed with pokers, which blended wonderfully with the skull and crossbones insignia on their hats. All of these clubs and canes were frequently used on the standees. Age or sex made no difference. They were especially brutal to the elderly, particularly the women. The sight of a beaten and bloodied Jew evoked laughter among the Germans.

There were also those who did not laugh. Just under my windows stood an SS man of captain's rank, approximately 45, handsome, of dark complexion, hair graying at the temples. He did not approach the group of SS and Gestapo men who were in the middle of the square. He smoked cigarettes nervously, lighting one after another, often throwing away half-smoked ones in order to start a new one. He unwittingly received my attention because he partially obstructed my view of the square. Next to him stood a giant SS sergeant, who chuckled without interruption and chattered incessantly, pointing out bloodied or beaten people. The officer did not smile even once, nor did he utter a word. After a while he approached Haase, exchanged a few words with him, saluted, and left the ghetto.

The shootings were increasing. New groups of people were brought to the square. The deportees clustered more closely. The heat was unbearable, people wore no hats, and had no luggage. They were taken as they were. There were those, I later learned, who purposely brought nothing with them so as not to be burdened on what would probably be their last journey. This time, there was a considerable number of Jews who realized what was in store for them. No one any longer believed in the legendary "Ukraina" and the Jews living there in camps.

After ten o'clock, acting on the orders issued, patrols of the Sonderdienst and SS, consisting mostly of four men, searched the apartment houses, apartments, attics, and basements. They broke open the closed doors with axes. Shots could be heard everywhere. There were howling dogs running through the crowded square, shouting of names, groans, wails, and laments after the last good-byes. Parting with old parents and children who were not permitted to go along—this was a hell which would never be forgotten. Mostly older people, and particularly men, held, in addition to small packages, prayer books wrapped in richly embroidered felt bags. Faith and devotion were not diminished. "God—where are you?" was whispered by some. "He is there," replied others. "God is on vacation, but He will be back," said one with a wry smile.

The shouts of the Germans were heard over the heads of those who were sitting. Occasionally someone in the crowd wanted to say something to the patrols standing by. Each such request was cut short by a hard punch, a blow from a gun butt, or a damaging kick. Above all of this loomed the tall figure of Major Haase, unmoving and remorseless. He looked at everything, surrounded by the staff of SS and Gestapo men—a lord—not of life—but death!

So many good friends passed before my eyes. I saw people with whom I had had long conversations; I saw the stubborn optimists and heard their political discussions, and those of their political opponents. They stood crowded against each other, poor and rich, old and young, men, women, and children. I saw the wife of Dr. Tiger, my neighbor for many years before the war, as she stood with her son, wearing no coat, in a summer dress, and without any luggage. Dr. Leon Gluck with his wife and daughter were there. He was pulled out of the transport at the last moment. I saw the industrialist Wachs, whom I mentioned before when I described the political discussions he used to have with Dr. N. Oberlender.

There was our daily guest, Dr. Schor. I saw Doctors Frederika Ameisen, Adolf Diestler, Fuchs-Katz, Amalie Goldman, Rachele Molkner, Adolf Kaiser, Gizele Gutmann, Barbara Rosenbaum, Zygmunt Leinkram, Stefanie Silberger, Ida Sperling, Stiglitz-Straucher, Jakub Weinstein, Wande Zaks, and Jakub Zabner. During the deportation, Dr. Jakub Kranz, director of a small hospital on Limanowska Street, perished heroically together with his very old sick patients. It would be impossible to list all the friends and acquaintances who stood in the square awaiting their uncertain future.

The squads of Sonderdienst and SS searched the apartments for hidden people. I heard the crashing of the axes on the doors, and the blasts of rifle shots. I sat alone in the closed pharmacy. The loud voices of the Germans, the cadence of their hobnailed boots came closer. My ears recoiled painfully from the bloodcurdling screams. I took cover in the frame of the door to avoid being shot. I could hear the steps of the soldiers just a few meters away from the pharmacy door.

The Germans divided their tasks—one went upstairs to the attic, the second walked down the hall, a third searched the basement, and a fourth stationed himself in front of the door leading from the hall to the pharmacy. The guard at the door bolstered his courage by firing his rifle. The blast of the shot reverberated through the deserted hall of the building. For his first search, he tried the door just across from my room. When I heard the cracking of the splintering wood, I decided to come out. In the semidarkness, I saw a short robust German struggling with the door. He did not notice me and did not hear my steps. I tapped him on the back and said, "Verzeihen" (Excuse me). As if shocked by electricity, he turned around terrified; apparently he could not understand how anyone could be here when the command was most explicit in its warning that anyone caught in the apartment after ten o'clock in the morning would be shot. I stood before him in a white pharmacy coat, which I had put on expressly to demonstrate to him the reason for my presence. However, he did not wait for my explanation; he saluted, turned, and departed quickly.

I returned to my room. Less than five minutes had passed when I heard the footsteps of several approaching Germans talking loudly. They came to my door. A loud kick—I opened. They entered: an officer of the SS, a subaltern, and two soldiers. They asked why I was there. I showed them all the pertinent documents. They inspected them cursorily. The subaltern explained that there could be no exceptions in view of the definite order. The officer, hearing the decisive tone of his underling, perhaps out of sheer perverseness, tried to prove to him that the documents were basically in order. In spite of my explanations, they took me with them. I came out and I was led to a group of Jews. The Germans left.

In the meantime, numerous people were brought in from all the streets and alleys. OD men scurried among the authorities, pulling themselves to attention and receiving orders. Spira stood straight in front of a high-ranking Gestapo man; Pacanower and Gutter bustled about subserviently. Förster, with his hand in his pocket, without an armband, moved around freely. From time to time he intervened with the Germans. Occasionally he was successful. The Germans permitted the exemption of one or two from the transport. There followed the most profuse thanks. The saved ones threw themselves around the necks of their saviors, crying with happiness.

I stood there, awaiting a decision. I trembled at the prospect that at any moment the deportation would start and then nothing could save me. After a while, SS Sturmbahnführer Haase calmly appeared in the company of the officer who had inspected my documents in the pharmacy. The Lieutenant motioned to me to come forward. The guard let me pass—I approached Haase, explained my presence, and showed my documents. These seconds seemed like an eternity to me; a slight wink from Haase, one little word, "Nein"—and I would share the fate of the Jews. Haase said, "I know about this"—and ordered me released.

I returned to the pharmacy as if from another world. I was extremely tired. I took up my previous post of observation, a small distance from the window, which was screened by a curtain.

I witnessed a scene which will remain in my memory for the rest of my life. Thousands of people were sitting and standing in Plac Zgody. Some steps away was a group of high-ranking SS and Gestapo men attired in impeccably tailored uniforms and highly shined boots. They held crops, clubs, or pokers. They laughed and joked continually. They randomly approached a group of Jews; to release some of their tension, they would beat and kick them. Many of these brutes' flushed faces glowed with frenzy. Suddenly a Jewish woman with a baby at her breast threw herself at the feet of an SS man, begging for her life. Next to the SS man stood Gutter. The woman cried, screamed, begged Gutter for help; she kept repeating her name, citing the occupation of her husband. Nothing helped; the OD man kicked her brutally and left. Not giving up, she ran after him, grabbed Gutter's hand

and pleaded. The German struck her several times on the head with his crop. Gutter nervously pushed the woman away, shouting mercilessly. The unfortunate woman fainted and fell to the ground. A member of the Sonderdienst grabbed her by the hand and pulled her and the baby back to the group. This was the only case I saw in which one of the Jews publicly pleaded for mercy.

Simultaneously, another scene played itself out. In the space between the pharmacy and the ranks of SS men walked a woman with a slow majestic stride. She was a pretty, nicely dressed young lady, wearing a light green cape. She passed close to the SS men but did not look at them. She continued, apparently wanting to approach the crowd of deportees. As we learned later, her mother was there. The surprised Germans gaped. One of them, the stoutest one with the most florid face, hands around his truncheon held behind his back, approached her and bent slightly forward. He had a wild expression on his face and eyes burning with rage. The woman stopped. He said something, she replied, and suddenly the German started to beat her. He beat her furiously about the face, neck, and back. I heard the sound of the blows in my room because the silence was deathly. The woman bent her head slightly and remained motionless, rigid as a statue. She volunteered for deportation to be with her mother, and this aroused the fury of the SS men. She did not moan or cry, she did not beg. The German could not break her—he could not force her to plead for mercy. Consumed with rage, he pushed, kicked, and shoved her into a group of deportees. She stood next to her mother; they did not exchange a word. The SS men left, she wiped her face with a handkerchief; her mother patted her on the head. Moments passed. The German approached her again, and said something. I did not see her respond. The German grabbed her by her hair, pulled her out of the line and screamed viciously, indicating with his truncheon in which direction she was to go. She was not permitted to remain with her mother—she was spared. This was the will of the SS. The woman left—she went slowly, helpless against the overwhelming power. The mother's gaze followed her for the last time.

That's the way it was. Germans were not privileged to hear groans, complaints, and lamentations in the Cracow ghetto, and that must have—in my opinion—enraged them the most. The spartan silence of the victims drove them berserk.

The other SS men who watched this episode were not moved in the slightest. They reacted as if this were the normally accepted way of treating these people.

The hour of departure approached. Many people—nearly 2,000—left their secret hiding places and came out into the street to be close to their dear ones. Those who remained hidden were safe for the time being.

During the October deportation, many of the sick and the invalids were liquidated—people were dragged from hospitals and nursing homes. Almost everyone from the shelter at Limansowska Street, which was headed by Dr. Kranz, was murdered. Those in the orphanage and the boarding school became victims to this heinous crime, as did the children who were taken from the Hospital for Infectious Diseases. Those arrested from the OD House of Detention, from Montelupich Prison, and neighboring camps were included as deportees. Especially cruel was the treatment of the elderly from the shelter on Limanowska Street. Old women and men, mostly invalids, were pulled out of bed and herded along the corridors towards the stairs. Beaten by truncheons and pushed—they were bleeding. It was quite evident that the condition of these people became deplorable and life-threatening. None of them—I later was told by Dr. Kranz—walked down in a normal manner. Almost all fell and rolled down the stairs. The Germans knocked the crutches out from under them and tripped them, laughing as usual when these indignities took place. In the courtyard they were lined up at the wall, ordered to jump, and the Germans would shoot them, laughing heartily. A natural death was not common in the ghetto.

During this deportation, there were many suicides. Several of the older people, at their fervent request, were given poison by their next of kin. One of the best-known doctors in the ghetto, radiologist Teofil Bluhbaum, unable to cope emotionally with what was going on, took fifteen grams of Luminal (one gram could be fatal). Not quite half an hour later, his relatives learned what he had done and tried to save him. In spite of the immediate pumping of his stomach, he slept for almost four days continually and only the unusual efforts of the doctors saved his life. He survived the occupation with his wife, and after the war changed his name to Murczynski and settled permanently in Szczecin. Dr. Czeslaw Murczynski had been honored by being named the rector of the university before the medical academy was created. His wife worked at the clinic. A number of years ago, both committed suicide. They were quite ill and partially paralyzed. In a letter which they left, they said that they were committing this act after long consideration, because they saw no purpose in further extending their difficult life.

I knew a certain woman doctor who had aged parents and an aunt. After their prolonged pleading and in an effort to curtail their torture during the transportation, she gave them cyanide. She told me about her plans in minute detail the day before she implemented them. After their last dinner with wine, after the final embraces and good-byes, when tears choked speech, three people's eyes closed in eternal sleep. The daughter carried the bodies to the courtyard of the hospital on Jozefinska Street and laid them there.

I knew a doctor who, at the urgent plea of his father, a very sick man, injected him with potassium cyanide. In spite of the large dose, death did not come instantly, as was expected; instead, he suffered a loss of consciousness and the terrible agony lasted for a number of minutes—apparently the poison had lost its potency.

A young SS man, Unterscharführer Horst Pilarzik, became notorious during the October deportation. His very appearance engendered terror. People hid inside. OD men met with him reluctantly. He was responsible for shooting a group of Jewish workmen returning to the ghetto from their jobs. He was the first one who dared to strike Spira in the face and beat Gutter with a truncheon. Later it was rumored that these atrocities had a calming effect on his murderous temperament. In a conversation with several Jews at the Madritsch shop, he stated, purportedly with a touch of repentance, that now he would be unable to shoot people, that he could not forgive himself, but that this was his first assignment since leaving a special school which he attended in Germany. He said that never in his life had he seen so many Jews in one place, at one time, as in the ghetto, and he shot without realizing exactly what he was doing. A strange explanation!

At about five o'clock that afternoon the Plac Zgody was empty. The Germans left the ghetto, the guards were relieved. This deportation was one of the most tragic and cruel. The workers who went to their jobs in the morning and left their dear ones in the ghetto found nothing but desolation upon their return. The broken apartment doors were mute evidence of the recent past. The blood on the steps, in the halls, and in the courtyards, the piles of corpses, and the absence of close relatives who left without a goodbye frazzled people's nerves. The crying and lamentations exceeded anything I had experienced in the ghetto thus far.

In some of the apartments, those returning from work found hurriedly scribbled farewell notes: "Don't worry about us; take care of yourself!" wrote mothers, wives, and loved ones.

People started looking for one another, each with a faint glimmer of hope that perhaps their dear ones were hidden somewhere, that they would still be found. They looked in attics, in basements; they pleaded with them to come out since the Germans had already gone. Unfortunately, those who were hidden were few in number. Friends and relatives embraced each other when they met, and silently wept over those who were lost forever.

Attempts were made to save the lives of those who had left. Perhaps the train was still at the station? Not a minute was to be wasted. The Germans were bribed: police, railroad men, commissioners; fortunes were promised, huge sums of money were offered, just to save relatives. Many telephone calls were made; cars left, driven by well-paid Germans. Even the German police were tempted. They drove to the railroad station, only to be told that: the train had left moments ago—did not stop at this station—was beyond the authority of the German in the car—or the destination was not known. In spite of the assurance of high-ranking Germans that this was the last deportation, no one believed them.

I remember after the Aktion of October 28, 1942, how keenly we missed Fillip Schor. We were very sad; we considered him lost because he was seen in a group bound for deportation. How great was our joy when, at about nine o'clock that night, the door opened and in rushed Mr. Fillip. He was very tired; asthma stifled any sound that might emanate from his throat, but nevertheless, jubilation was reflected in his tired, sickly face. After a short time he revived, laughing like a small child, dancing and singing. He had never been so happy. "Well, if they didn't get Fillip this time, they never will," he said mournfully. In fact, they never did kill him. Some weeks later he contracted pneumonia; gravely ill, he dragged himself to the pharmacy in an almost semiconscious state. He never appeared again and after a few days he died, as he would have wished—in his own bed. His wife and daughter obtained a permit to go to the cemetery. His body was carried in a hearse driven by the good undertaker, Pinie Koza.

The October Aktion resulted in 7,000 unfortunates deported, and about 600 killed on the spot. The faith of the optimists who hoped to survive the war was badly shaken.

Late one night, a registered nurse from the gynecological hospital, Mrs. Erwina Order-Panzer, who was the right-hand assistant of Mrs. Dr. Feniger, came to the pharmacy. Everyone in the ghetto knew sweet Mrs. Erwina. Always smiling, full of empathy for the needy, she was a woman of an exceptionally cheerful disposition. She sat on a stool, supporting her tired head on her hand, tears streaming from her eyes—she slowly told this story in a low trembling voice. A few hours before, she had lost her beloved mother. The Germans put her in a railroad freight car at Plaszow Station, transported her out with the others—although she could have saved herself. While she was walking through a crowded street filled with people on their way to Plac Zgody from where the deportation was to take place, she heard moans coming through the window of a small house on Jozefinska Street and she followed the voice calling for help. Apparently a young woman was giving birth and was unable to come out to the street. Mrs. Order's mother decided to stay with the woman in labor until the end. After some hours, the Germans, together with the Jewish police who were searching the apartments, came upon the woman in the throes of delivery and Mrs. Order's mother. A short command was shouted: "Take her too." No explanation helped. She pleaded that the mother had the right to remain in the ghetto, that her daughter worked in the hospital, and that families of those working in the health department were protected. "Raus, los, schnell," screamed the Germans maniacally.

The people returning from work did not realize what was happening in the ghetto during their absence. Going into the street invited death. When Mrs. Erwina discovered what had happened to her mother, she ripped off her armband and, taking advantage of the confusion in the police station at the intersection of Limanowska and Lwowska Streets, left the ghetto. She ran wildly toward the Plaszow railroad station in pursuit of her mother, to where the train with the deportees was to leave. She looked and called for her mother. She rushed from one train to another . . . unfortunately the one she was looking for wasn't there; no one would say anything. She returned to the ghetto because her sixteen-year-old younger sister, Halinka, was there. Halinka also was in a group of deportees on Plac Zgody. I saw from the pharmacy how, at the last moment, an SS man pulled her out of the crowd and pointed her in the direction of an exit. He let her live a while longer. She ran toward Targowa Street. Halinka survived the war. Just a bit of luck, an uncharacteristic, momentary display of goodwill, a whim decided her fate.

The Cracow Jews perished without achieving a libertarian revolt on the scale of the Warsaw Ghetto Uprising, but they died with dignity, honorably, and without abasing themselves before the enemy. With the exception of a small number of those who sold out to the enemy, all who worked in various capacities engaged in deliberate and effective sabotage. Everything possible was done to slow the tempo of the assignments, to fail to meet deadlines and, in the ghetto, to remove valuable objects, destroy and burn them, so that they would not fall into German hands.

A Jewish Fighting Organization (ZOB) functioned in the ghetto. They worked closely with the underground groups outside the walls. Some of these heroes of the resistance I knew and some of those with whom I was not personally acquainted were: S. Dranger, Szymek M. Borowski and his wife Justina, A. Liebeskind, Dolek Abe, Jan Ropa, Laban, Abraham Leibowicz—"Romek," one of the leaders, Golda Mirer, ZOB contact with the Polish resistance movement, Rajza Klingberg, Han-Balsamowich, David Herz, Roman Bromberger, Moniek Eisenstein, Icchek Zuckerman, "Antek," one of the leaders of the Warsaw Ghetto Uprising, Bauminger, Halbreich, Warszawska.

The accomplishments of this organization included many acts of sabotage and divisive tactics against the German conqueror.

In October of 1942, the members of the ZOB set fire to several loaded trucks, truck-trailers, and gasoline tanks located in the military barracks at Grzegorzecka Street.

On November 2, 1942, an attempt to assassinate the Gestapo informer, Marcel Gruner, and his wife occurred. Formerly, they lived in the ghetto, later outside the walls. The plot failed then, but they both perished later, after the March deportation, on order from the secret organization. During this action, one of the members of the group, Robert Offner, also died. Another warranted exploit of the ZOB was the execution of Adams, of the Department of Press and Propaganda of the General Government.

In September of 1942, the ZOB started to publish a Polish language journal, entitled *Democrats' Voice,* in a printing of 40 copies; about 60 issues appeared subsequently.

In October of 1942, the assault division GL, to which the "Iskra" (Spark) of the ZOB belonged, under the command of Jakub Halbreich, set fire to a garage on Wloczkow Street, in which were stored three cars and barrels of gasoline.

Idek Liber headed Iskra in December of 1942. It bombed the coffee house Cyganeria on Szpitalna Street in Cracow on December 24, 1942. Eleven Germans died in this attack, and 13 were seriously wounded.

One of the leaders of the ZOB in the Cracow ghetto, Adolf Liebeskind, was surrounded by the German police in one of the bars on Zulawskiego Street. Shooting ensued. Liebeskind killed two Germans but, realizing that his situation was hopeless, he took his own life with a bullet from his revolver.

One of the centers of the ZOB was situated outside the ghetto at 10 Skawinska Street. One morning the German police rushed in and arrested everyone there including the leader Abraham Leibowicz. They were all transferred to the camp in Plaszow and shot some time later.

The name of Szai Dreiblatt is inextricably linked with the active conspirators. He lived in the ghetto and devoted all of his spare time, from the start, to construct a bomb, using only the most primitive of tools in a locksmith's shop. Of course, under such circumstances, the attempt failed. The only thing smuggled out of the ghetto was his detailed design, which was used later in the production of the bomb. His conception was used in preparing the munitions for the attack on the premises of Cyganeria in Cracow, previously mentioned.

CHAPTER 4

—Camp in Plaszow— Another Contraction of the Ghetto Area —Execution in Plaszow— Verified News of the Fate of the Deportees —Ghetto A and B— Ghetto Inhabitants from Outside Cracow —An Attempt to Close the Pharmacy— Further Restrictions —Organizing of a Kinderheim—

After the October deportation, news about the establishment of a camp in the area of the former Jewish cemetery was circulated for the first time. Every day, scores of Polish workers were leveling the ground. After a while, Jews were also assigned to the work. The more valuable monuments, especially those of black marble, were dug out and stored. Lumber for the construction of the barracks was brought in, sanitary drainage was installed, and wells were dug. The entire area of the works was proscribed by wooden posts; barbed-wire guard towers, so characteristic of concentration camps, were erected.

People started to wonder for whom the barracks were intended. The ghetto was again rife with gossip and guesses. The most "reliable" German soldiers left no doubt that they were for Poles; others said for the Jews from France and Hungary; still others were sure that they were meant for all the young men from Cracow who would be billeted there. Discouragement and apathy dominated the mood after the October deportation.

In November of the year 1942, the news was confirmed that the camp was being built in Plaszow for the Jews of Cracow, and that the days of the ghetto were numbered. Its fate was sealed. People were worried and, at times, indifferent. Confusion and questions prevailed. What will happen to me, to my relatives? What of the children?

Some became psychotic, others were constantly tormented with anxiety, still others suffered from deep depression, incapable of logical thinking about their immediate future.

"Sir," said a frequent visitor to the pharmacy, pointing toward the window facing Plac Zgody, "you tell me why there are so few 'crazies' after all that these people have been through. Are the brain cells so resistant to all those disasters these people have experienced? After all, before the war there was no dearth of insane people, and what misfortunes did they suffer that compare with our tragedies?"

After a while, he spoke again: "What do you think would happen if suddenly, let's say today, the war ended? If people regained their freedom, would all of them go berserk? I often think how it would be, and I really do not know. How happy I am to be alone, that I don't have anybody in the world. And still, I am not indifferent to this environment, I live with these people, I learned to like their children, and they became a part of my family. How strange is all of this."

In the hearts of all of those who were still alive, there probably was a small glimmer of hope that they would survive, and the thought persisted that some one of their relatives who had been deported would miraculously survive and return. My friend survived and visited me.

"And yet, I don't feel happy in the true sense of the word," he said, lowering his voice.

Pressing my hand, he looked into my eyes for a long time and, upon leaving, promised that he would not forget me, that he would write to me when he had settled somewhere permanently. He said good-bye and left, but he never wrote.

Under these conditions, after the loss of one's relatives and feeling lonely, time started to heal the wounds, even the most grievous ones, and those who, just a short while ago, forswore starting a family and tying themselves to someone for life, started to change their minds after the war. They began to seek new partners, entered into new marital relationships. Life, it seems, is stronger than resolutions.

Even in the ghetto, immediately after the terrible ordeals were over, those who survived sought mates to rebuild their lives together. Rabbis who had hidden in the underground sanctified the new marriages.

And in the ghetto, the Arbeitsamt completed the files; new jobs were created; there was talk about billeting people who worked in the same shops in certain blocks in the ghetto, so that they would not have to commute. Obtaining a pass, even for a bribe, became more difficult; people feared and distrusted others. In the meantime, the construction of the Plaszow camp progressed.

In November of 1942, after the deportation, another contraction of the ghetto area was ordered. Now it became clear why the decision had been revoked in October. The streets eliminated from the ghetto were the left sides of Lwowska, Dabrowska, and Janowa Wola.

The inhabitants received 24 hours' moving notice. Again those scenes of unbelievable horror were rampant. The crowding was incredible. Several families who were incompatible were assigned to one room. This exacerbated the dismal mood, frayed the nerves, and drove some to madness. Constant quarreling about the quantity of household goods brought in, about the size of the space occupied, about the kitchen, and who was responsible for setting the fire in the stove, how to store the coal jointly, who had greater right to the apartment—these were the objects of daily contention. For the first time, moving was permitted throughout the night. Lights were turned on in the ghetto from early evening. Traffic was insufferable. Unending lines of people loaded down with everyday necessities were stretched far in both directions. Simultaneously, Jewish workers fenced in the new ghetto boundaries. Again, no walls were erected; instead, posts were put in place on which barbed wire was strung. This type of obviously temporary enclosure of the ghetto confirmed suspicions about its impending liquidation.

Apartment houses were crammed with accumulated furniture. In the courtyards were enormous accumulations of closets, credenzas, and night tables—in the halls and in the outside passageways were piled great quantities of trunks, bundles, and junk. No wonder that in all the confusion many items were constantly missing. Every day someone would open another person's valise or package. Coal was lost, bedding and food disappeared. Mere existence became almost intolerable, nightmarish.

Living with others in a shared apartment became increasingly difficult. When several families occupied one apartment, the common kitchen was the usual place for fierce arguments among the tenants. At the height of these oral outpourings, I heard such remarks as: "Hitler knew how to wreak vengeance on the Jews, and so he created a ghetto into which he crammed so many people." Heating a room occupied by several people became a source of conflict. No one was willing to share the cost for coal, arguing that it was warm enough, and that more heat was not necessary. Such quarrels were maddening. I knew of a case where tenants of a certain apartment, unwilling to yield in their arguments, stubbornly froze all winter long, despite the fact that there was plenty of coal in the basement. Another bone of contention was the furniture. Everyone wished to move loads of junk. The scarcity of space would not allow for the placement of the least amount. However, those who moved in first occupied the largest areas for their furniture. Those who followed fought bitterly for a bit of room. They complained and cursed. The pettiness and attachment to material possessions dominated even in the most dire of circumstances.

Kennkarten were invalidated, and the Jews were forced to use the *Judenkart* (Jewish Pass) instead.

The ghetto was reduced in size in the prescribed time and the moving was completed. Tremendous amounts of belongings had to be left behind. All of the empty apartments were sealed off with all their contents. The German and blue police patrolled the deserted streets of the former ghetto.

Special details of workers, composed of Jews from Arbeitsdienst, started to sort things out. Pieces of furniture were carried out to the street, where they remained for weeks on end, rotting from the rain and cold. A directive in the daily official organ of the German authorities, dated November 14, 1942, created five closed ghettos in the area of the General Government: Warsaw, Cracow, Lwow, Radom, and Belzec. All other localities were declared "Judenrein." The order urged every Jew who resided outside of the ghetto to return there. A faint hope glimmered for some. Again the Germans were victorious in their swindle, in their clever perfidy. Many returned to the ghetto; others were discouraged from leaving the ghetto by this directive, their vigilance was so weakened that they would become sitting ducks for the brutality which ensued.

The constricted ghetto continued to exist, in spite of its strange, unnatural life. People's vitality was diminished, but they continued to live. People left for work daily for the construction of the Plaszow camp. The future manager of the camp, Amon Goeth, who succeeded Mueller, pushed the men to work faster, constantly threatening to shoot those who slowed down. As evidenced later, his threats should have been taken very seriously; murder and the death of others were, for him, a sporting indulgence. He rushed the Judenrat, threatening severe penalties for negligence in executing orders. Workers who left each day frequently did not return at night, but were billeted in the camp. These were the first compulsory inhabitants of the Plaszow camp.

One somber day after the October deportation, the acting head of the Judenrat, Gutter, and the director of the OD, Spira, were ordered to attend a conference at the SS and the police headquarters on Oleandry Street. They returned from that meeting late at night. The discussion must have been very special, because the secret proceedings demanded that the lips of the participants remained sealed. From the expressions on their faces one could guess that they had not heard anything good. From the brief and guarded utterances one could gather that something big was about to happen; this time, however, outside of the ghetto. That night I was visited by one of the Judenrat functionaries. I learned then what had been discussed at the meeting in Oleandry. It seemed that the following day the Judenrat officials and the majority of the OD were to march out of the ghetto toward Plaszow and there, near the railroad station, await the Gestapo. What was most interesting was that they were told to bring rope, several meters long, and talcum powder. It was not too difficult to guess what these were for. There would be an execution; they would be hanging someone, but the most torturous question was—who? There was even a possibility that it might be one or more of their group. Anxiety pervaded the long sleepless, nightmarish night. People tried by any means possible to disobey the order and remain in the ghetto. Doctors' certificates were used to excuse the absent. Very few succeeded.

Next morning, lined up in columns of four, the Judenrat and the OD, with Spira and Gutter at the head, marched out toward Plaszow. In front strode the OD man Feiler, a curious figure, big, broad-shouldered, slightly stooped, a man of about 46, with the florid face of a drunkard, married but no children, arrived in the ghetto from the provinces. He could not speak in a normal voice; he shouted as the Germans did at everything and everybody—always a little tipsy, seldom drunk despite the fact that he drank a daily tot of a half liter of one hundred ninety-five proof alcohol. The liquor probably seemed weaker to him with each passing day. He was quite a simple man, semiliterate, speaking mostly only Yiddish, a little Polish, and even less German. Still, he communicated excellently. The Germans understood him and he them. He relished their sympathy. Because of his looks, and his ability to drink alcohol by the glassful, he had a great rapport with the Germans, one which only he was permitted to have. Feiler would pat an SS major or a Gestapo man on the shoulder, speak to them in a raised, hoarse voice, negate and often express opinions contrary to theirs. Nothing ever happened to him. No one ever struck him. He simply entertained the Germans. He was by nature unusually nervous and extremely excitable; he would fly off the handle quickly, for no apparent reason, become furious, his bloodshot eyeballs almost popping out of their sockets —he was unbelievable. He would scream like mad, thrash about with his ever-present short stick, cursing his victim and using the crudest obscenities. He was a man who was not quite normal, but basically good. He was never in the service of the Germans. He did not even want to remain in the ghetto after its liquidation, but left with the others to the camp at Plaszow, coming back to the ghetto every day. He suffered deeply about the injustices and the misery of his associates, crying like a baby after each execution—he was capable of taking risks, and occasionally he was successful in receiving mercy for someone. But Feiler was an OD man, the same as Spira and his cronies, and yet he was so different from them in his impulses and his actions. The Germans liked and trusted him, but somewhat differently than they did the other OD men. They never proposed spying or informing to Feiler. He knew how to maintain discipline and obedience, and he knew how to execute German orders without causing personal harm to anybody. In the Plaszow barracks, he was entrusted with the care of the storage of Jewish possessions. His direct superior was Untersturmführer Popek. Feiler was slain, supposedly shot during a dispute with an Ukrainian, but in truth Popek shot him intentionally and with premeditation on the order of higher authorities, most certainly as an embarrassing witness. The autopsy was performed by Dr. S. Lewkowicz, a surgeon in the camp hospital in Plaszow, and it was ascertained that the bullet that was removed came from a German revolver and not, as the Germans said, from the rifle of a Ukrainian. This, however, did not prevent Balb from later offering condolences to Feiler's wife on the death of her husband. He promised to severely punish the perpetrator and to reprimand him. As for the wife, he permitted her to continue to occupy her present apartment outside of the camp in the barracks next to the stores. No one was surprised, though, when after about a week had passed, Mrs. Feiler was thrown out of the barracks and ordered to live in the general camp. This Feiler, then, was the detachment head who shouted commands to maintain order and marching pace.

At night everyone returned. Mystery surrounded this strange expedition. The secret could not be kept for very long in spite of the strong German prohibition. By nightfall everyone in the ghetto knew that on orders of the Gestapo in Plaszow, prisoners brought from Montelupich were hanged. The gallows were erected near the railroad track, and an inscription over them proclaimed that this fate awaited everyone who committed sabotage. The sentence was carried out by Jews. No one knew who these prisoners were. They were transported in a canvas-covered truck. Their hands were tied behind them; some looked like they might be Poles, others like Jews. Under threats of death, it was forbidden to exchange even a word with the condemned. After warnings about further acts of sabotage and the fatal consequences for those who committed such acts, they started to carry out the sentence.

The prisoners were lined up on boards under the gallows. The Jews were ordered to cut the rope, put the nooses around the necks of the victims, and, at a given command, pull the board out from under their feet. They were all hanged at the same moment above the ground. I received a detailed report that same evening about the execution from one of the participants at the horrible executions, the honest OD man Rottersman. Many Jews had much for which to be grateful; as he told me, this entire spectacle was photographed in the minutest detail by the Germans, who would offer the pictures as propaganda to prove that Jews were murdering Poles. Similar executions were repeated in a few weeks.

Since the first hangings, many OD men started to drink—mostly pure alcohol, but the cases of uncontrollable drunkenness were infrequent. People who never drank before sought relief in liquor; the nerves of many started to deteriorate. Insomnia became a common malady.

An extremely clever man, Oskar Feil, lived in the ghetto. He was able to help himself quite handily in difficult situations. When he talked of his exploits, he really enjoyed himself. He was proud of every time he was able to make a fool of a German. He applied for a job as a specialist mechanic for the repair of typewriters and calculators, and he was first employed by the Gestapo and later in the office of SSU Polizei on Oleandry Street. While working on the machines, he would request various spare parts, which he requisitioned from the German warehouses which were stocked with equipment seized from Jews and Poles. He would go there, guarded by a German policeman. There, he would pick the best parts of new machines, and with an escort, go to a mechanical workshop located on Florianska Street, which belonged to a Pole, Molodecki, who knew what it was all about, would pay cash for the parts brought in, and give Feil old junk, which he later threw out. Small repairs were supposed to be made in Molodecki's shop. And all this was happening in the presence of a German policeman! In this way, Feil managed to sell several new typewriters and one calculator. Another one of his tricks occurred during the time of the issuance of the so-called Blauscheins, when people stood in line for days on end in the unbearable heat, uncertain as to whether they would receive the paper that was tantamount to being sent on deportation. Feil, after some brief cogitation, took a ladder, which stood next to the line, and, pushing himself through the crowd, entered the building, calmly climbed the ladder, and started to work on an electric box; by the way, he knew nothing about electricity. After a while, he came down and, holding the mechanism on his shoulder, he handed his Kennkart to one of the Germans, who unwittingly handed him the necessary blue card.

In Plaszow, Henryk Goldschmidt, a draftsman by profession, who, like

Feil, went with a guard to the SSU Polizei to draw on the large wall of the office in Gothic letters the slogan, "IT IS QUITE UNIMPORTANT WHETHER WE LIVE, BUT IT IS IMPORTANT THAT OUR RACE, THAT GERMANY, LIVES." He worked on this trash quietly and calmly for several weeks until some police pundit realized that, after all, it was not fitting that a Jew should inscribe such lofty aphorisms, and the whole project of painting slogans was scrubbed.

In November of 1942, a letter arrived in the ghetto from a female relative of one of the doctors, who had run away immediately prior to the October deportation and had journeyed to Lwow. Her route led through Belzec. I had this letter in my hand and read it to my coworkers. The news of its contents spread through the ghetto like wildfire. It was, one could say, the first authentic confirmation of what was heretofore only rumored, in various versions, of the fate of the deportees. The author described realistically the trains filled with people, stationed in Belzec for days awaiting destination orders. This meant moving the transport to a side branch of the railroad ending in a deep woods surrounded by fences and barbed wire. The area over the forest was enveloped in thick smoke, and an unusual noxious odor pervaded the air. The inhabitants of Belzec said that the deportees who lived through the ghastliness of the transport in the closed cars remained for days at the station without a drop of water or a morsel of food. Moans and cries for help came from the cars, but assistance was forbidden. German police guarded the train. When it arrived in the woods, the guards opened the doors, and those still alive had to strip and were herded into gas chambers; then their bodies were cremated, and so the smoke hung heavily over the area. The letter ended with an appeal that no one be deceived about the fate of the deportees. Whoever could should escape as soon as possible, before it was too late. This news engendered a terrible mood in the ghetto and destroyed the last lingering shreds of illusion.

Again rumors of a new deportation began to circulate. It was said that Plac Zgody would be cut off from the ghetto. And once more people were buoyed by this news: they thought that if the Plac Zgody were eliminated, then the deportations would cease because there would be no room to carry them out. The authorities' announcement about the creation of five permanent ghettos in the General Government seemed to confirm these guesses. Small wonder that under these dreadful living conditions, and after experiencing all those horrors, people frequently reached implausible conclusions. Of course, they were invariably wrong.

At the beginning of December 1942, surveyors appeared on Targowa

Street and Plac Zgody; maps in hand, they staked out borders and made some measurements. The ghetto was to be divided. No one knew anything for a certainty. A few days later we learned that the ghetto was to consist of two sections. Trucks delivered poles and barbed wire. Salomonowicz and Ing. Gunter, members of the Judenrat, marked out the bounds of the two areas.

On December 6, the ghetto was split into Ghetto A and Ghetto B. Then a directive ordered the workers living in Ghetto B to transfer to Ghetto A and vice versa; all non-workers from A were to move to B. The line of demarcation ran directly across the front of my pharmacy, which landed in part B, to which the inhabitants of A had no access.

Again, the moving started, the looking for new quarters and carrying the remnants of one's possessions. This time, virtually no one took any furniture; people destroyed such furnishings by hurling them from the upper floors to the courtyards below to break them into pieces for firewood. From early hours, the courtyards echoed with the crash of closets, credenzas, tables, and chairs. Ghetto B's population decreased daily. Conversely, in Ghetto A, the squeeze was intensified. Some days later the transit between Ghetto A and B was halted. OD men were stationed at the gate which divided the two sections, carefully guarding the boundary. To get from section A to the pharmacy, one needed a pass from the OD. At first this was fairly easy; in time, however, it became increasingly difficult until, finally, an order was issued forbidding it absolutely. People in Ghetto A were now completely cut off from the pharmacy. Almost no one came because part B contained the unemployed and the indigent. To solve the problem of supplying medicines, the OD performed a service to the pharmacy by delivering the prescriptions to the people waiting behind the barbed wire. The turmoil was intolerable; nonprofessional people were making mistakes, especially in the dark, mixing medications and filling prescriptions, relaying the names of drugs incorrectly—real madness. On orders from the SS, the role of the OD was transferred to an employee—a runner of the Judenrat who was ordered by the German authorities to wear a cap bearing the inscription "Apotheke." From this time onward, he was the intermediary between us and the customers. He was paid for this activity by us and the Judenrat. He was a bright boy who learned quickly; as a result, the mistakes ceased. Everyone liked him. He was always smiling and well-behaved, so that, in time, dispensing medications through the barbed wire did not present any grave difficulty for the customers. We were probably the only pharmacy in the world which, for a period of several months, was visited by only one person. This boy's cap with its inscription, "Apotheke," could be a unique exhibit in a museum of Polish pharmacology. On the 13th of March 1943, the day of the liquidation of the ghetto, this situation was ended.

Jews from the surrounding small towns were brought to Ghetto B. They were figures in tattered garments, barefoot, hungry, infested with lice, with faces unshaven for a long time, with dazed expressions in their eyes, terrified. They occupied the empty apartments and buildings. The majority of them had never been anywhere outside of the villages where they were born; they had never seen a larger town in their lives. I did not know whether they were aware of what was going on around them, whether they even realized that a war was being waged, that there existed a Hitler, an SS, a Gestapo. There were many such people in the building that housed the pharmacy; I tried to get closer to them, to find out more. They lumbered like bears in a cage, continually shuffling along the barbed wire, begging for bread from the passersby on side A. They had nothing with them; their entire belongings consisted of the dubious contents in their torn pockets. Many were barefoot, and this was in the midst of winter, frost outside, cold in the apartments, and the water in the pipes almost always frozen. These people slept on the floor; it was a blessing if they found some straw. Their hands and feet were frostbitten, sores covered their bodies, scurvy was endemic, they itched with skin diseases. We helped them as much as possible. We dressed their wounds, helped those with frostbite; we shared our bread and served hot tea to which we added some alcohol. Each of their little pathetic smiles was a token of their heartfelt thanks. The OD forbade them to leave the building. Hunger, however, proved to be stronger than any command or threat. The OD, being unable to manage them, nailed the gates and windows shut so that no one could get out into the street. Once, sometimes twice daily, they were served food like wild beasts in cages. They grabbed it, and without chewing, swallowed it in large chunks. In a minute there was no trace of food to identify what they had eaten.

Everything made of wood was burned. In the building where the pharmacy was located, any trace of wooden closets, tables, and chairs disappeared. In a few weeks the handrails, the stairs to the basements, doors of empty apartments, window frames, and even floorboards were broken out and burned. To get to the attic or basement at this time was almost impossible. Worst of all, the water pipes burst, sending water down the walls and flooding rooms. No help was possible because no one was permitted to enter Ghetto B. I finally succeeded in obtaining a permit for a mechanic to come in and shut off the water. A pharmacy without water—it is not necessary to describe how the sanitary closets looked in a building where several hundred people were shut in without water. After the ghetto was vacated, the front of the outhouses located in the courtyard was littered with mountains of filth reaching a height of a meter or more. Occasionally, and sometimes twice daily, the OD men prepared lists of people who lined up in the courtyard and gave their names and professions; all this was written down on special forms. Some of them pretended to be specialists without the slightest knowledge of their stipulated profession, in order to save themselves.

The year was 1943—a very harsh winter—great sadness in the ghetto. Weeks were already being counted to the time when it would be necessary to leave their apartments in the brick houses, to take leave of their belongings, and to begin to live in the wooden barracks on the hilly dunes of the Plaszow cemetery. But this was not the most important worry. What would happen to the children? How widespread would be the relocation? Would everyone go? These were questions which continuously occupied their minds, causing sleeplessness.

The Arbeitsamt divided the working population of Ghetto A into three divisions, marking them with signs: "R" (*Rüstung*—Armaments), "W" (*Wehrmacht*—Armed Forces), and "Z" (*Zivill*—Civil). The three insignias, on a triangular piece of cloth, bearing an SS and police stamp, were sewn on the left side of the jacket at chest height. This was an obligatory complement to the Judenkart. The Arbeitsamt stopped fulfilling its usual functions, which emerged as the exclusive power of the SS and police. Henceforward, they directed the Jews to their employment or barred them from their jobs.

The camp in Plaszow was enlarged. People said that special barracks for children were being erected, and that even a kindergarten would be included. There was talk that stores would be built and that the character of the ghetto would not change. There would be no more deportations, and enough room for everyone. It was not difficult to guess who authored this gossip, who was interested in lulling their suspicions. There were people, albeit not many, who really believed all of it.

Life in the ghetto seemed routinely normal. But this was not a quiet life. Almost daily, trucks arrived. SS men organized posses; they roamed the streets, seizing people, beating and kicking them, regardless of age or whether they worked. At the sight of these trucks, the streets became deserted; everyone hid in the buildings for hours on end.

There were plenty of friends in all the rooms of the pharmacy, particularly in the back room, from which it was easy to escape through the rear exit. It was difficult to grasp that we were the fortunate, that good luck would favor us in the critical situations. Where did all the informers hide? The basements and attics were occupied by fugitives as well.

Days passed under the fear of deportations, the constant chases, arrests at night, and the transports to concentration camps. In the pharmacy we were visited by our friends who found a way of getting to us; every day there were discussions about Frank's latest speeches or the current war communiques; from these observations, chances of survival were evaluated. Conclusions were reached. They believed that some of the Jews would survive, since they would not be able to murder all of them. People sighed longingly, in the nostalgic memory of a fairy tale, at the thought of the day of freedom, when the Germans would flee. Just to live for that, nothing more—just to see them ruined. Even the desire for vengeance was neutralized. The underground papers raised their spirits. There was another source for the secret press, Antoni Krawczyk, whose son was shot in front of the synagogue at Szeroka Street.

The first and only fire in the ghetto occurred in January 1943. A store and a warehouse which contained paint and turpentine were engulfed in flames. A woman on the second floor jumped out of a window; the fire brigade came—the fire was extinguished.

On the 15th of January 1943, after I returned from lunch, I was informed at the gate by the OD man stationed there that the Commissioner of the German police, Bousko, wanted me to report to him immediately. I found out from Bousko that Sturmbannführer Haase from the SSU Polizei had just visited the ghetto and ordered the pharmacy closed. No one was permitted to enter. I was terrified and asked for advice. There was only one solution: Haase could change this directive. "You have no alternative," said Bousko. "Early tomorrow go to Oleandry Street and present your case to Haase."

My situation at this moment was hopeless—I considered it impossible to obtain a change of an order from Haase. However, I decided to take the chance.

The next day, I first went to the appropriate authority, the Health Department. The German officials in the Gesundheitswesen were relatively sympathetic toward the Cracow apothecaries, and, besides, it was easy to come to an understanding with them utilizing the known methods. The value of the argument with which the petitioner supported his case was not that great. A bottle of perfume, the largest size of nylon stockings, a bottle of vodka, a box of cigars—it was easy to reach an agreement. And so it happened. Loaded with the above "arguments," I presented my case and received the required papers for the SSU Polizeiführer. It stated that closing

Hard labor in the Plaszow camp

the pharmacy would endanger the health of the inhabitants, that Jews deprived of medicines could become carriers of disease and epidemics whose rapid spread could not be stopped by ghetto walls or barbed wire. The next morning I went to the lion's den. I reported to Haase in the waiting room. The door of his office opened and the murderer of thousands of people appeared before us, and in all his uniformed resplendence, announced in a flat voice that the problems connected with the ghetto could be dealt with only by his specialist for Jewish affairs, Kunde. Kunde, however, was not there. The next day I entered Haase's chancellory and met Kunde, whom I knew quite well from the ghetto. I handed him the papers, and in a few words I presented my request. He led me to his office, asked me to sit down, and offered me a cigar.

The discussion began—Kunde regretted the outbreak of the war and was sorry about the many victims, but he faulted our prewar government. He told me that as a husband and the father of two children, he was suffering from the separation—he showed me pictures of his parents, his wife, and children. He spoke to me about his loneliness for the homeland, about the beauty of Cracow, and said that when the war ended he would live here permanently. He stated that, as all Germans did, he loathed the Volksdeutsch, that they were swine: they were like chameleons who changed color at the whim of the wind. He expressed his sympathies for the Poles, adding that in his opinion, many would gladly become Reichdeutsche, if this were possible, but never Volksdeutsche. He did not understand the politics of certain people who considered Poles as being of a lower order, while he considered people only as decent or bad. He spoke about everything but my papers. After this monologue, because only he talked while I listened (I was absolutely at a loss to understand Kunde's behavior), we finally came to the business at hand. After he read the entire memorandum from the Gesundheitswesen, and asked me several questions—among others, he tried to persuade me that my name was not a Polish one—he filled out proper forms and passes for me and my employees to enter and leave the ghetto at any hour of the day or night. These were yet to be signed by Haase. I waited a while. Unfortunately, Haase did not sign the passes because, in consideration of the new more stringent regulations regarding the complete isolation of the Jews from the Aryan population, the passes could be validated only on a guarantee for me from the Gesundheitswesen. I left without understanding what this meant. How could the Germans write a guarantee for a Pole? The Gesundheitswesen did not understand it either. What did the SS want? They telephoned at length, spoke with several specialists—and—I ran around the city buying presents. Finally, the papers were completed. I attached to them a guarantee written by myself, in my name and those of my employees. I promised that I would not have any contact with the Jews, that I would have no conversations with them except those that were necessary for dispensing medicine, that I would not allow German or Polish newspapers in my premises, and that I would not engage in political discussions or help the Jews.

The next day I waited for Kunde from eight o'clock in the morning till noon. When he arrived he was as polite as he had been on the previous day. I handed him the required addenda and I waited for his reaction. After a few minutes I received the signed passes, valid for fifteen days. I risked handing him a bottle of whiskey; he did not accept it. He said that when he would pass by the pharmacy on some other occasion, he would drop in.

My duty room was privy to many interesting and mysterious visits. There Kunde arranged meetings with certain individuals. He did not want to bring them to his office located in the same building where the Jewish police was housed. Many secretive figures, various informers from different cities and towns, passed through this room. Almost every one of the visitors wore dark glasses and each spoke German fluently. None wore an armband. The conversations were low, so that they could not be understood through the door. Such sessions usually lasted approximately thirty minutes. Two individuals never arrived at the same time. They came punctually, so that a few minutes after one left, another appeared.

One morning, and this was a Saturday, on a beautiful but hot sunny day, I emerged in front of the pharmacy. I was astonished to see a young lady coming through the gate of the guard house. She was trim, dressed in black, her face half-covered by a black veil and she wore no armband. At a slow pace she approached the pharmacy. She entered, lifted the veil and asked me if I were the owner. "Yes—that's me," I answered. She slowly removed a long black glove, shook my hand, and introduced herself, saying, "Mrs. Roniker. Kunde asked me to wait for him here." I led her into the room and she sat down. I offered her a cup of coffee—she accepted. After a few minutes, Kunde arrived and they chattered idly. I slowly retreated from the room but I did not completely close the door behind me. The conversation became more animated, increasingly loud on the part of one party. The subject was the "fixing" of the arrest of a certain man. Several times the name of a very well-known Cracow doctor, Kazimierz Piotrowski, was mentioned. He was a popular gynecologist, theater critic, and a knowledgeable man of many interests. A close relative of the doctor was probably involved. The mysterious lady reproached Kunde: "How do you operate? Why did you break your promise? This business was supposed to be attended to long ago." Kunde made excuses for himself and his colleagues. After an hour of talk, cups of black coffee, and several glasses of vodka, they left. She said good-bye and thanked me for the refreshments.

In the same room, an unusual event took place, a black humor prank. One afternoon, Kunde dropped in holding handcuffs. He said, "You know what, let's play a joke on the ladies in the pharmacy." "What kind of a joke?" I asked. "I will handcuff you and then we'll walk out of the pharmacy together so that the ladies will not see us—we will go there," pointing to the corner of the building across the street. "There we will hide from their view—I will shoot my revolver—take off the handcuffs and we will come back. The ladies will think that I shot you. It will be fun," he said. A macabre jest, I thought, when he handcuffed me. After a while we got up and left. My ladies, petrified by horror, thought the worst. We stood behind the corner of the building. Kunde pulled out his revolver—I offered my soul to God, not sure of what would happen in the next moment. He shot into the air, put away the revolver, took off my manacles, and, laughing, returned from the alley. I must confess that I did not feel very much like laughing. It would be difficult to describe what was going on in the pharmacy in the meantime. My ladies were sure that I had been shot. However, the bizarre jest had a happy ending.

The start of the year 1943 was not a very happy one. In compliance with the latest orders from Berlin about the strict isolation of Jews from the Aryan population, a further directive was issued forbidding Jews to pass in the streets bordering on the Aryan sections and separated by barbed wire. All the stores on those streets were subject to automatic liquidation unless they had an entrance from the courtyard. The traffic there stopped completely. The stores and the building gates were closed. Sometimes, only an OD man could be seen on the deserted sidewalks. The ghetto was closed and completely concealed from the view of the people outside. It hid its own mystery, zealously guarded from the world. A notice was posted inside, ordering the Jews into the barracks in Plaszow. The commander of the future camp exerted pressure. He charged the Judenrat with ever new, extremely difficult or impossible tasks: for instance, they demanded that the disinfecting shop at Jozefinska Street should process, i.e., bathe, barber, and disinfect 300 persons daily. The manager of the shop, Mgr. of Pharmacy Raschbaum, told me how, at a conference of the SS, he was severely reproached for sabotaging the German regulations because of the slow working pace of the people in his shop. He proved to the Germans, with statistics, the physical impossibility of carrying out their orders; to which they replied that the quota had to be raised by fifty people, and if he did not fulfill it, he would be shot.

The Gestapo was actually unwilling to agree to the liquidation of the ghetto, or in any case, they tried to delay the process. Complete abolition of the ghetto and the relocation of the Jews to the barracks in Plaszow would deprive many of them of lucrative positions in the General Government, or even expose them to the possibility of being sent to the front.

The camp in Plaszow became populated. At first the carpenters, bricklayers, locksmiths, and all those who were involved in the construction of the barracks were billeted there. Every day, new regulations and orders specified the tasks and stipulated their deadlines, after which the workmen, following a delousing, were to report to the barracks; the orders stated that only those possessions one could carry were permissible. Liquidation of the ghetto became a reality. It was only a question of time until this tragedy finally ended.

In the ghetto, a Kinderheim—children's home—was opened by order of the Germans. At the opening ceremonies, Gutter and Spira were present. It was quite an occasion. New lies, new swindles, again designed to discourage vigilance. Parents going to work could bring their children there to the age of 14. Cared for by experienced personnel, the children would be busy with all kinds of tasks, such as sealing envelopes and weaving baskets. In addition, they were taught sewing, to help adults in communes when the ghetto moved to the camp. The Kinderheim was filled every day with scores of children who entered willingly and with joy, without even the slightest hint in their innocence of the immense danger and tragedy that was imminent. Just imagine that all this was done just for the few weeks before the preset date for the murder of all the children who attended the Kinderheim. But the children worked happily and the parents were pleased with their elation and with their progress.

CHAPTER 5

Transports to the Camp in Plaszow—Liquidation of the Ghetto—March 13–14, 1943—Psychological Puzzles—Murdering of the Sick and the Children—Nightmarish Scenes

And so the days passed by swiftly, each one similar to the one before in their hopelessness and filled with the most dire forebodings for the future. The population of the ghetto lessened each day. Almost daily transports were sent to the camp in Plaszow. In the first weeks, the changes were not so noticeable because the crowding of the people in relation to the number of buildings was tremendous.

They started billeting people who worked not only on the barracks in Plaszow, but also those who were employed in many other shops beyond the ghetto area, as the "Emailfabrik," the airport and cable, workshops at Montelupich, Zentrale fur Handwerkslieferungen, the clothing manufacturing firm of Julius Madritsch (Podgorze's Main Square 2), Deutsche Rustungsfabrik in Zablocie, the prefabricated barracks shop in Zablocie, the brick factory in Bonarka (suburb of Cracow, same as Zablocie), the military automobile shops, the Gestapo workshops on Pomorska Street, on the Wawel (Wawel-Burg), and the city sanitation department. Only in a few of those places were the Jews billeted. The others were brought in under close guard and were returned to the camp in Plaszow after completing their work. Long columns of people could be seen—wretched and abused physically and mentally; filing slowly through the streets of the former ghetto; there was sorrow and pain in their lusterless eyes. How much disgust, how much contempt every human being must have felt towards the Hitlerites who were capable of using so many terrible ways to torture people. "Today, you and tomorrow, perhaps us"—a thought which must have entered the minds of all logically thinking persons when they gazed at the lines of people looking more like ghosts than living human beings, glancing about for some acquaintance, a relative, or a friend. Every day, those behind the walls of the camp and those who were purportedly free would bring us news of new beatings, arrests, and deaths.

The first transports left for *Julags* (Jewish Camps)—small camps in Plaszow, Prokocim, Bonarka.

The first doctor from the Cracow ghetto who was sent to the camp in Plaszow was Dr. Leon Gross. He later became a chief camp doctor, elevated to that position because he was the first one who came to Plaszow. The Judenrat, in the meantime, delayed going "upstairs" to the barracks. Each day an assignment "downstairs" meant that one could possibly survive; going "upstairs" made people tremble with fear. At that time the number of OD men in the ghetto was reduced considerably because many left for various posts in the camp. To fill their places, other ghetto inhabitants applied because the demand for OD men was always heavy, and in that job there was a hope of saving oneself and one's dear ones. The approval or rejection of the candidates was the responsibility of Spira. The aspirants had to pass an examination; this consisted of coming to attention before Spira at a distance of two meters, saluting, and in a loud, assertive voice, calling out one's name, duties, and readiness to serve. This had to be done in Polish and German. It was the entire examination. Spira's mood, the proper "support," and one's appearance were the deciding factors in the selection.

Life in the ghetto was becoming increasingly worrisome. The fear of liquidation was always present. Every day someone would leave. People said good-bye to each other, their apartments were vacated—only small valuables were taken. In the OD offices, the German specialist for Jewish affairs officiated from early morning until late night; many papers were filled out and, accounts were written, as were reports of the hearings of the prisoners from the ghetto jail. Almost every day someone escaped from the ghetto. The stores disappeared gradually. No one replenished missing stock any longer, and current merchandise was rapidly being diminished; people literally lived from day to day, and spent whatever they made. The Judenrat, with Gutter at its head, tried for several successive days to postpone the date of the liquidation, using whatever means possible. All attempts failed. Haase refused to agree to a delay of even one day. On the 13th of March 1943, at eleven o'clock in the morning, the Judenrat, by order of commander SS Obergruppenführer Scherner, publicly advised all that by three in the afternoon, the inhabitants of Ghetto A would be marched to the camp in Plaszow, and on the following day, Jews from Ghetto B would be directed to the train stops of the Ostbahn. The Sonderdienst, composed of Lithuanians, Latvians, and Ukrainians, and the blue police surrounded the ghetto; some police units entered and occupied positions at the transfer points from Ghetto A to Ghetto B along the entire boundary line. The people who crossed from Section A to B did not encounter any problems, but those from Section B were unable to get to Section A.

The general mood was somber. Nervousness was extreme; the street traffic was impossible to describe: shouts, people running loaded down with possessions, looking for their proper places and for their relatives. There were only a handful of Germans in the ghetto, encircling the streets. They were led by Amon Goeth, automatic in hand. He and his staff, together with his ever-present dogs, Ralf and Rolf, intensified anxiety. The OD men ran about crazily. The hospitals were being liquidated.

Looking through the pharmacy window, I saw everything come to an abrupt halt; no one shouted, no one spoke, the silence of the grave hung like a pall. All eyes looked toward Targowa Street. "Someone must be coming down the street, someone terrible," I thought. Actually, it was Amon Goeth who appeared—tall, handsome, heavyset with thin legs, head in proportion, and eyes of blue, about 40 years old. He was dressed in a black leather coat, held a riding crop in one hand and a short automatic rifle in the other; close to him were two huge dogs. OD men snapped to attention before him. Seemingly not looking at anyone, he crossed the Plac Zgody and turned into Solna Street and disappeared. Everyone relaxed and continued to move toward the exit gate. Various dignitaries arrived in the ghetto by car in order to intervene for their people and to guarantee their safety. There were Heinemayer, chief of the political division of the Gestapo and his deputy, specialist SIPO Koerner. Some German cars departed with the rescued ones. Marcel Gruner and his wife left in a furniture van, with his possessions and furniture. Koerner went out with two doctors. Rumor had it that later they escaped to Warsaw, and from there to Hungary. We were witnesses to all of this.

The Germans were experts at creating an atmosphere of panic, horror and fear. We could hear the blasts of gunfire and the unpleasant sounds of whistles, the howling of dogs, and the screams of the Germans. The fear of losing their children deprived people of their reason. Some hid them under beds, locked them in closets or other ingenious hiding places. Many children wandered aimlessly in the streets as if bereft of their senses, seeking help from strangers in vain. Parents did not know what to do. The time for leaving was imminent; it was impossible to take the little ones along. In a group ready to go waited husband and wife; others wanted their grown children to go with them. The Germans assured everyone that all the little ones would go "upstairs," but later, after the grownups. It was well known that a special children's barracks was being built in Plaszow.

The doctors leaving the hospital informed the patients of the order of the Germans forbidding them to leave their beds. However, they did call attention to the danger of remaining in the hospital. "Everyone who can," they said, "should try to save themselves." A panicky exodus of the patients ensued. Anyone who could stand left the hospital. The postoperative patients departed, the old and even the young, people with high fevers, as well as the convalescents. I saw how from the epidemic hospital, in a small alley off Plac Zgody, sick people in their underwear ran in all directions. It was a horrifying spectacle. With their last vestiges of strength, falling again and again, rising with pain, they continued to crawl. Some were accompanied by their families. No one knew what to do with these people. They could barely stand, but to cross the gate they had to maintain a healthy posture so that their illness would not be apparent. However, not all were able to flee the hospital; some were unable to lift themselves; these remained, knowing what to expect. There were the last good-byes, the last requests and notes for relatives—and then tomblike silence.

In the ghetto, the feverish rushing and the frantic scrambling in all directions persisted. Whoever could, hid and squirreled away their most precious possessions. We carried out the valuables of our friends to addresses in the city in accordance with prearranged plans. We could not keep too many things in the pharmacy because a search could take place at any moment. In the empty pharmacy drawers we temporarily placed all kinds of things, some valuable, others of no consequence except as memorabilia to the owners. No one asked for receipts or worried about how the objects were kept. Only the honesty of the receiver was relied on. Each one hoped that in time they would be able to sell the stored items and use the money to make life easier in the barracks. Many suffered from extreme hunger as a result. From our pharmacy, all kinds of packages and correspondence were directed through Dr. Michal Weichert, the Director of Jewish Social Self-Help, which supplied medicines and food to the Jews in the Plaszow camp and to many other locations outside of the Cracow area. Those who received our help trusted us implicitly. The ladies who worked in the pharmacy fulfilled their requests and instructions, often at the risk of their own lives.

However, not everyone who accepted these items for safekeeping would return them at the owner's request. With shame, we frequently had to tell the prisoners in the barracks who requested their valuables that they were gone. We would embarrassingly explain there had just been a search and that their valuables had been confiscated, or that they could be returned to only the owner (it was generally known that this was impossible because no one could leave the camp). In spite of verified, handwritten requests from the owners, return of the valuables was refused.

On the other hand, there were many decent people who did return everything entrusted to them and who cared for the things left with them as if they were their own. Occasionally some would help with their own means.

The moment for resettlement was drawing near. People lined up four abreast in close groups, bundles in hand, ready to depart. They waited only for the order. Everyone wanted to be "upstairs" already. They were tired of the constant uncertainty. Almost all of them considered the barracks in Plaszow to be the end of the journey, the last stage of their wandering. It seemed to those poor unfortunates that the barracks were finally permanent. They were convinced that there would be no more deportations—"Whoever endures will live" was the general belief.

There was one matter which was most disturbing: the fate of the children, a problem still not settled, uncertain and worrisome. In the Judenrat, the Germans officiated; there were continual consultations which resulted in the issuance of orders that the Jews were enjoined to scrupulously obey and implement. Members of the Judenrat left the Council building, preceded by the Gestapo and SS men. The terrible news spread through the crowd: children were forbidden to enter the camp. The news hit the parents like a thunderbolt. It seemed that this decree was new—no one anticipated it until now. Yet, it shouldn't have been because it was repeated after each deportation; it was the constant torment of all parents with small children. People continually deluded themselves and lived through these painful disappointments. This time was no exception. Ever present was the belief that the special children's barracks were being erected. They also believed in the permanence of the recently created Kinderheim, and the trust in the solemn German promises that all the children would be together with their parents in the barracks "upstairs." Even now, the Germans did not rescind their promise—they only changed the date. The young would not go now, but after the grownups marched over, they would follow in cars. The children would be placed in the Kinderheim. This time, many of the concerned ones believed it.

Many mothers distrusted the Germans, did not have faith in their assurances; they were not willing to leave their children alone. They therefore left the ranks of their group and went over to Ghetto B, whose existence was calculated to last another 24 hours. Most all of the men remained in the ranks, surrendering to the persuasion of their wives; they deceived themselves into believing that they would be able to do something for their dear ones; they expected a miracle. The women who remained were the nameless heroines of silent sacrifice, noble and courageous. Unforgettable impressions of those poignant scenes were indelibly etched in the minds of all who witnessed them. Total strangers cried, observing the pain of those who remained in utter helplessness. This was a thousand times more horrible than the physical torture and murder of the defenseless. Children, wandering about, were seized and led to the overcrowded Kinderheim.

In the pharmacy we survived hellish scenes. People, petrified with fear and agony, broke down completely. More acquaintances came to tell us that a husband and wife who remained in the ranks could not decide to leave the child alone and decided to stay together. Everyone had something to say. It is difficult to describe our leave-takings—the last embraces—and softly spoken words of thanks. Beloved dogs of good friends remained with us. The poor creatures, sensing that something was wrong, were sad, did not eat and whined.

Breathless people rushed into the pharmacy to get Luminal for children, to put them to sleep, so that they could be carried in a backpack as luggage, or to take them to a hideout, unwilling as they were to go to the barracks. We were busy dispensing anti-cough drugs.

Many children had Luminal and codeine to thank for their lives. On that day, a great number of people managed to get to the "Aryan" side.

The gate of the ghetto opened. The first groups walked out. Germans stood at the gate and carefully watched so that no child should pass. Children who were detected were brutally torn away from their parents. If either father or mother chose to remain behind with their young, they pushed the child away and separated them from the parent. Children at the wire looked long and tearfully after the departing parents.

New details were continually heard. Someone was killed, another beaten to a pulp, patients were shot in the hospital. In the Aktions, two Gestapo men vied for first place in brutality—Hujar and Frommer. The first was a fat, red-faced monster, who ate apples ceaselessly, and would shoot at anyone in his view. Frommer executed the Aktions singlehandedly and quite differently from Hujar, who became excited by the sight and close proximity of his boss, Goeth. Like a crawling dog, he circled his chief and, with downcast eyes and a revolver in his thick hand, would intuitively guess his thoughts and orders. These were the two who, with innate sadism, would spot children in the dense crowds leaving the ghetto and brutally snatch them from their parents' arms. In every case, the parents were mercilessly beaten, and the children, in mortal fear, in the cacaphony of the unbelievable screams of the mad Germans, would run away in panic, hiding in the doorways of nearby buildings. Many of those expelled in such fashion came back to the barbed wire and looked intensely at the people awaiting marching orders. The poor little ones clutched the wire with their tiny hands, and with tearful eyes, fear and indescribable sorrow, whispered, "Mommy, Daddy, don't go away, don't leave me alone here, take me with you." During the liquidation of the ghetto, several of our close friends did not want to leave to live in the apartments prepared for them a long time ago on the "Aryan" side.

My coworker, Mgr. Irena Drozdzikowska, offered one such location near Wieliczka to Dr. Leon Steinberg and his family. Unfortunately, he delayed his decision for so long that the liquidation of the ghetto made his escape impossible. Dr. W. Armer also had such an opportunity for his family but he also waited too long. When a suitable apartment became available, the risk of escaping to it was far less than the risk in the Plaszow camp. In spite of that, the desire to stay in the group with the others, among friends suffering the same fate, was, in many cases, most compelling.

Late in the afternoon, the last inhabitants of Ghetto A departed, with the exception of the OD, Gutter, and a few members of the Judenrat who were ordered to stay until the complete liquidation of the ghetto was effected. At the last moment, Dr. Weichert was exempted from leaving for the barracks because the Committee for Social Care of the General Government ordered him to stay to continue to be in charge of the business of JUS (Jewish Social Support Agency).

On the very busy streets where just a short while ago each building, courtyard, or gate reverberated with the hum of human voices—suddenly, there was silence. Deserted apartments, open windows, barren streets—a frightening void!

With measured steps, the German guards paced the dividing line between Ghettos A and B, separated by barbed wire.

No one was in the streets in Ghetto B. People hid in empty buildings, no one dared to come out. Anyone sighted, even through a window, meant certain death. The Germans were waiting for just such an opportunity. The silence was often broken by the sound of shots of the German patrols. I looked through the window and saw a German standing just behind the barbed wire in front of my pharmacy, aiming his rifle at my windows. I pulled back—a shot rang out. The sounds of a closing gate—scattered voices—approaching steps could be heard. After a short while, a group of people from the hall leading to the pharmacy brought in a wounded person. I opened the door; it was a woman about 45 years old, pale as a ghost. She was the mother of five children, all young. She had lost her husband in the June deportation and was left alone with her children and without permission to remain in the ghetto. She hid during each Aktion and escaped detection until that day. "I won't break down now, either," she said. "What bad luck, just when I must be strong." She tried to run from one building to another to reach her children who were hidden in an attic. Suddenly a German spotted her and his shot wounded her badly in the shoulder. She was hit by a dumdum bullet leaving her shoulder blade fragmented and exposed. The hole in her back was the size of a child's head. The wounded woman did not moan, for now she was numb, in shock and faint. We started to dress her wound despite the fact that her clothing was deeply imbedded in her flesh. Fortunately, after a few minutes an OD physician, accompanied by a guard, arrived. He was Dr. Armer, a wonderful man, who finished dressing the wound and gave her an injection. The woman was hopeful that everything would be all right. She had to live. "After all, I have to save my children," she said, and asked how long it would take for the wounds to heal. We consoled her by telling her that she would be better in a few days, but we knew that in her condition it was doubtful if she could survive. Later we lost all trace of her. She was probably shot together with her children.

During the evacuation of Ghetto A, a great number of people devised unusually clever methods of escape—albeit very dangerous: they would lift the covers leading to the main sewer crossing under the streets of Podgorze. People descended and, loaded with bundles, often holding children in their arms, wading to midriff or higher in filth in which rats scurried.

There were two such sewers: one at the junction of Jozefinska and Krakusa Streets, and the other at the crossing of Jozefinska and Wegierska Streets.

Old and young, women and children ran away and, but for a betrayal, this route could have saved the lives of many. One of the first to go into the sewers was Dr. Aleksandrowicz; with his wife and his little son, he slogged for hours through stinking waste. The sewer end was at a large outlet to the Vistula, close to the railroad bridge. I remember that day as if it were only yesterday. Julek Aleksandrowicz rushed into the pharmacy like a bull, revealed his plan of escape, which was to take place in a few moments, handed me a thick briefcase containing his scientific works, and asked me to hold onto it. Then, the last handshake, the last kiss, tears in the eyes and . . . so sad. His escape from the ghetto and his family's adventures are related in the book *Pages from the Diary of Dr. Tough*, published in 1962 by the Literary Publishing House.

After a long time, someone (after so many years, I do not remember who it was) came to me with an authorization for the return of the briefcase. When I handed it over, I asked about Julek. I was told that he was not alive, that he had been shot. I understood perfectly well from the narrator's wink that this was supposed to be said, that it was to remain the truth about Dr. Aleksandrowicz's demise until the end of the occupation.

The first daredevil escapees triumphed. The exit was safe—there were no German guards nearby. However, this situation was shortlived. Betrayal doomed the fugitives. Reports about the escape of the Jews were telephoned to police posts; shortly thereafter the sewer outlets were surrounded by police, and the unsuspecting escapees were caught by the Germans. In many cases, as they emerged from the outlet, they were shot on the spot.

The night of the 13th to the 14th of March was horrible. Ghetto A was completely liquidated. All the close and casual friends were gone. As they took their leave, they advised us to flee because the Germans might decide to liquidate us as embarrassing witnesses. In Ghetto B people were fearful of the following day. No one had any illusions about the fate of those who remained. After all, these were the nonworking people, and as such, were expendable, including women and children. No one slept that night. People walked like somnambulists in the halls, basements, and the attics of the apartment houses at Plac Zgody. At dawn, as in previous deportations, the square was soon filled. Gaunt figures emerged, muttered to themselves, unshaven, unwashed, with dazed expressions on their faces. Resignation and terror were rife. Women with children in their arms or in carriages appeared. Old men shuffled carrying prayer books and ritual shawls in satin bags under their arms. Children alone holding each other's hands could also be seen. The day was beautiful, warm, and sunny. The youngsters sat down quietly on the asphalt; they laughed, playfully beat each other, fought about toys, and then cried again. The crowd grew—the square was jammed. Next to those who were standing were piles of packages, bundles, bedding, and household items such as pots, pans, dishes—they seemed to be prepared for a long trip, taking whatever they could with them.

I was frequently asked in the company of my Polish acquaintances whether the Jews were so oblivious that they could not realize what was in store for them. Why, knowing that they were to be deported and would be killed, did they take these things with them? Why, on their final journey, did they even bother? Why didn't they resist in self-defense? Why did they let themselves be led docilely like sheep to the slaughter? Such questions could only be asked by people who were not eyewitnesses of these events, whose information was received obliquely and not quite completely.

Anyone who did not see at firsthand the awesome horror could not understand or grasp the dire circumstances that plagued these people. They could not fathom the perfidious lies which misled them the day before their death. If my questioners could spend even a few hours in the funereal atmosphere in which these Aktions took place . . . At every few steps someone was killed, beaten, humiliated, and tortured. If one could look behind the scenes of these crimes and see the perpetrators, observe the means they used to instill fear and terror, cruelly shooting, and deceiving the "resettled" with a hope that they would live; if the inquirers knew about the threats of revenge on the entire family for even thinking about escape, for sabotage, and for any self-defense action—he would no longer ask "why." Besides, unlike the Warsaw ghetto, for instance, the Cracow ghetto could not be utilized for any resistance effort because of its geographic location. Compact and limited, a score or less of streets were patrolled by the German police; the fact that even a casual glance could reveal any activity inside was not exactly conducive for any large-scale conspiracy or armed rebellion. Besides, the Germans, preparing for a deportation, were well-organized to ensure their own safety: they stationed experienced police units in the ghetto, fully armed and with the option to shoot anyone at any time.

After all, deep in the heart of all glimmered, however weakly, the hope of survival. Survival—that was a wonderful word in those days; could there be anything more desirable in that time of travail and bondage than freedom, and in the ordeal of bloody carnage—survival? This hope was miraculous; it imbued people with superhuman power and endurance and enabled them to withstand the basest humiliation. Not the fear of death but the will to survive was the dominant instinct. This was my impression arrived at in those fateful days as a result of my experiences in the ghetto.

I tried to delve deeply into and understand the psyches of individuals and groups of people with whom I was in contact at that time, and I arrived at the conclusion that, if it were any different, all those who were shot would have begged for mercy, humbled themselves or tried to flee. Such behavior would be unquestionable symptoms of fear and cowardice that certainly were absent in the Cracow ghetto. I did not hear any pleading, whining, or crying. People faced death calmly, resignedly, and proudly. The Germans did not see their terrorized victims whimpering and sobbing for mercy.

The units of the SS and the Sonderdienst entered through the gate of Plac Zgody. They lined up in a double row, armed with rifles, helmeted, tall, well-built sons of the "heroic" Herrenvolk. Cars arrived with various dignitaries. The soldiers stacked their rifles in front of them. The ghetto looked like a town preparing for a battle. Again, in front of our windows, scenes very similar to the previous ones the time of the last Aktion were enacted. The only difference was that this time the murdering was greatly increased, as if for the finale the Germans wanted to sate themselves in blood. The shooting from early morning was incessant. Everyone who wanted to shoot did so.

Oberscharführer Albert Hujar, with, a jeering grin on his bloated face, burst wildly into the main hospital at Jozefinska Street and started to shoot every patient in sight. Running amok like a rabid animal through the entire building, leaving a trail of blood and corpses, he shot the guard at the gate and the dog cowering in the doghouse. He charged into each ward and murdered everyone lying in bed and all those he met in the halls. He ran into the cell where sick prisoners were transferred from the OD to the hospital and shot them all, though some were well enough to return to the barracks.

In one of these rooms, the crazed Hujar found a pretty young woman lying in bed. Next to her stood Dr. Katia Blau, who did not wish to leave her friend Mrs. Berger. Mrs. Berger had tried to flee through the sewer. Holding her little son Fredziu in her arms, she fell and broke her leg. A German caught her and brutally seized her child. She would never see him again. Moaning in despair and in pain, she still managed to stretch her hands before her, like Niobe when she lost her sons, and, as if she were talking to herself, fell in a dead faint. She was transferred to the hospital. The dedicated Dr. Blau, a beautiful blond with sapphire blue eyes, stayed with her. One could imagine the worry these two endured, hearing the shots and the menacing steps approaching their room.

Hujar, as if in a trance, stared at both women, looking penetratingly from one to the other, and with small steps he approached them holding a cocked pistol behind his back. When he neared the two women, he hissed at the seated Dr. Blau and ordered her to get up and turn around. Dr. Blau realized instantly that she was doomed—but she had won the battle and emerged victorious as a good woman, a caring doctor, and a human being.

"Shoot, I am not afraid of dying"—these were her last words. A shot rang out. Miraculously, the death of this woman saved the life of the other. The German did not shoot the woman in bed and returned the gun to his holster. The OD man standing by was ordered to transfer the patient to the hospital in Plaszow. A while later, her spirit broken, Mrs. Berger committed suicide. The loss of her beloved little son was more than she could bear.

In this gory hospital Aktion, two physicians were also murdered, Dr. Jan Fischer and Dr. Bruno Palin. After the liquidation of the ghetto, the doctors who survived were relocated to the camp in Plaszow. Sometime later we learned that Dr. Wladyslaw Sztencel was slain in Plaszow and Stanislaw Eibeschutz was deported in one of the transports to Belzec and met his end in the camp crematorium.

News also reached us about two well-known engineers in the ghetto area, Grunberg and Morgenstein. They participated in all construction activities in the ghetto, including the rebuilding of hospitals and delineating the frequently changing boundaries. Both were murdered on Goeth's order.

New groups evicted from their homes came running. The Germans rousted them from all sorts of hiding places, basements, and attics. Not all the German policemen shot those they discovered on the spot; many victims still suffered a great deal before meeting their ultimate fate. In the square, the Germans shot, beat, and tortured their victims by prearranged plan. Foreign citizens with foreign passports, who until now walked about freely in the ghetto, and the prisoners kept at the OD, were shot in a blind alley leading from Plac Zgody to the epidemic hospital. I saw a frail, bearded Jew who was a Hungarian citizen and was known in the ghetto as a vendor of Star of David armbands was allowed to move freely in the city but did not take advantage of this privilege. However, in spite of the existing ruling, he did not shave his beard. He came running into the square, with his papers in hand. Kicked and beaten, he fell to the ground, arose, fell again; he stretched out his hand with the papers to an SS officer and stood before him. Without reading the documents, the officer destroyed them. He then ordered the Jew to turn around and pointed him toward the street. At the corner, he killed the man with a shot in the back of his head. Many people perished in that alley at the wall of the building located directly in front of my windows; old men were lined up and shot; they were mostly people pulled out of hiding; in another corner, they murdered children. Planning, even for committing crime, is the requisite policy of the Germans. We saw a large group of old women being herded, prodded, beaten, and wounded in a narrow alley, Wit Stwosz. Shots echoed—they were slaughtered.

People paralyzed with terror remained silent and calm while awaiting their turn. They were resigned to their fate. If not here, then surely in a few hours they would die.

At Jozefinska Street, the Germans started to liquidate the Kinderheim. Wagons arrived into which the children were loaded; the small ones were thrown into baskets and carried out to the wagons, several at a time. The older were led to the square and shot at the corner of the blind alley.

Throughout the continual segregation of the younger and stronger-looking from the rest and amid the seemingly endless beatings and shootings, high dignitaries of the SS and Gestapo remained unperturbed, chatting with each other as if nothing were happening. Sturmbannführer Haase, surrounded by his staff, was in complete command. Goeth circled round. Oblivious to the pitiful screams, whistles, and the barking dogs, Heinemayer, the ever-present Kunde, Heinrich, Olde, and many newly arrived Germans who were unknown to me passed in front of me.

The SS men started to line up the crowd facing the exit, separating the women from the men, taking the children from their mothers. All this was done with unbelievable cruelty and inhumanity. Like the sadists they were, beatings and murders apparently stimulated their eagerness for new thrills. They arranged a race of death. It all happened in front of my windows. In the square, they randomly selected people and placed them in groups. These were mostly men who were more than 60 years old. They were told to run forward as fast as they could. The outcome, they were told, would decide whether they lived or died. Amid jeering and laughter, the wretched victims ran, at first individually, then in groups. The SS men shot at them. The fast ones saved themselves temporarily. The SS men patted them on their shoulders, praised them for their fast pace and for their good condition and endurance, then ordered them to turn round and shot them in the back of the head.

The color of one's eyes, the shape of the nose, the expressions on one's face quite often decided life or death. I saw a man, about 60, who refused to run. He walked quietly, without looking back. Open disobedience made the Germans wonder; lack of fear of death impressed them and drove them to frenzy. They did not shoot him, but kicking and beating, pushed him into a group destined for deportation. This was their vengeance, because they knew what agony awaited them before they died.

There were, however, many who were saved in these races. They were considered fit for work and were included in a group of young men. Arranged in fours, they were to be transported to the Plaszow barracks. Some of them left immediately, others remained until the authorities decided. They were kept in the OD until the general deportation from Ghetto B. They were then assigned to the removal of clothing from corpses and loading them on flat cars.

In all, 150 men were selected. Goeth reported to Haase that he was taking all of them to work to Plaszow. Haase, after some consideration, said, "Too many. Cut it in half." Seventy-five men were shot, the other half stayed on.

The time for departure approached. We became aware of this when the bundles were seized. Everyone was ordered to leave everything behind. This time the Germans left no illusions about their fate. This time there were no lies and deceptions. They were no longer necessary, because this was the end of the ghetto. The SS men brutally seized even their handbags and threw them on one big pile. At times someone would complain that his personal papers were in the bags. Even now, if only for a moment, people still deluded themselves into believing that they would live, that the papers would be needed, reactions similar to the death twitches and convulsive quivering of a hanged man.

Heavy freight trucks arrived at the front gates. The crowd swayed, rose from the ground. People squeezed through the open gate. SS men standing in the passage yelled like maniacs, kicking and pushing people to the exit. Cries of the separated children and screams of the parents froze the blood in the veins. Children were left in their carriages to meet an uncertain fate. The parents accurately guessed what lay in store for them. The shooting did not stop for one moment. Time and again, a new group of Germans led children to the courtyard of a building which was not far from the pharmacy, as I mentioned before. A series of shots left no doubt about what happened there. People fled the ghetto in a rush. They would quickly climb into the trucks because the SS men standing by were beating them mercilessly. For many, this kind of scrambling presented great difficulties. Their relatives helped the elderly and women, in spite of the blows on their backs and heads. Bloodied and wounded, with black-and-blue marks on their faces and with mouths full of blood, they jammed into the trucks.

In the throng in the first row I saw an old woman sitting on the ground. She had fallen asleep, apparently from fatigue, because she did not react to the shouts of the Germans ordering everyone to vacate the square. She sat motionless, probably in a faint. I saw an SS man approach her slowly, bend forward, hands behind his back. How alike they all were while committing murder! They employed the same movements and gestures. He held a revolver in one hand, came to within a few steps of her, extended his arm, aimed and shot. I saw the old woman jump up as if struck by lightning, stretch and open her arms. A second shot rang out, this time the bullet hit its mark. One more killed!

Some trucks crammed with people left; others came, taking new groups.

The square was emptied. The liquidation of the Cracow ghetto was drawing to an end. In the Plac Zgody, as on the battlefield—thousands of bundles, luggage left behind, and, here and there, small children played on the asphalt wet with blood. The SS men took the children's hands. Occasionally a German led several of them, holding each other, to that nightmarish courtyard. Others pushed carriages in which babies slept. Each such procession was followed by a salvo of shots. For economic reasons, several children were shot with one bullet by lining them up in a row. Several babies were placed in a carriage and killed with one shot. In the square, Haase and his staff were in absolute control. I saw A. Goeth, W. Kunde, K. Olde, Heinrich, K. Heinemayer. With his legs spread wide, constantly wiping sweat from his forehead, stood the hero of the hospital Aktion, A. Hujar; next to him, gesticulating in a lively way, was Frommer.

I saw how the OD man Immergluck led his old mother. As a token of recognition for his dedicated service in the OD, he was permitted to accompany his mother. He covered her with a blanket, gave her last directions for the journey, embraced her, and smoothed her hair. The farewell—a long, seemingly unending kiss, the son's tearful eyes and the infinite terror in his mother's face. When he left the square walking slowly, she stood with her arms outstretched as if she wanted to embrace him once more. The Germans stood nearby, but somehow this time, they did not laugh. Several hours later, the son was stripping his mother's clothes and carried her still warm corpse to the platform where the murdered were collected. Thus, she was saved from deportation.

That day about 3,000 people were deported. Haase reprimanded Gutter for not advising the authorities about the large number of inhabitants in Ghetto B. Nearly 1,500 people were murdered; the SS man Hoering reported to Haase that approximately 1,000 were killed.

The ghetto died, and it would seem that this was the last act of the tragic drama. However, the Germans were able to devise even more debasing methods to torture those still alive. This time they defiled the ultimate dignity of death. After the last German units left the ghetto, the ODs and the remaining Jews were ordered to strip the murdered ones completely, then to deposit the corpses in the doorways of buildings, and later to load them on platforms and carry them away.

I saw how old and young were unclothed, women and men. Dresses were taken off the infants. The bodies were placed one on top of another. In many cases sons recognized their parents among the dead; parents were forced to strip their own children! Trucks entered the ghetto, nude bodies were thrown on. I saw bodies shot with dumdum bullets directly into the face, leaving a gaping bloody black hole and hair matted with blood. Not infrequently the wounded were thrown on the loaded trucks with the dead bodies. I saw a moving truck full of corpses, and among them a woman who quite visibly was raising her hands to her face. The moans of the severely wounded could be heard when the trucks passed the exit gate of the ghetto. The trucks, loaded to the limit, were covered with blankets before entering the streets beyond the ghetto area, and so, dripping with the blood of the murdered, they rolled like butcher wagons through the narrow streets toward Plaszow. In several instances, corpses fell out because of the broken pavement on Wielicka Street.

Each hallway left an unforgettable impression. In the pools of blood were mired bundles, packages, and parcels of food prepared for the last journey. Next to them were discarded items of religious ritual wrapped in velvet—prayer books, kittel (prayer gowns), and prayer shawls, strewn about by the Germans looking for treasures.

A funereal stillness enveloped the depopulated streets and the deserted houses of the ghetto. Every corner and every street were now gaping voids. Every alley seemed to curse the nation that created so many criminals. Everything in the ghetto, even the smallest memento cried out; each spot was an indelible reminder of the infamy of the Hitlerites.

Two women doctors, well-known in Cracow, were transferred to the camp in Szebniach during the March deportation: they were Paulina Wasserberger, for many years a physician with the Cracow Insurance Company, very active socially, and her sister, Dr. Dora. They were both killed during the liquidation of that camp. Several weeks after the demolition of the camp in Plaszow, we heard the sad news about the murder of two other well-known doctors, Bertha Silberberg and Dr. Maria Pechner.

During the annihilation of the Cracow ghetto, individuals and entire families perished, often very large familial groups whose ancestors settled in Cracow hundreds of years ago and whose names were recorded in the ancient chronicles of the old Cracow. With their demise, the genealogy ended and the traditions vanished.

Respected names like Holzer (banker), Wohl, Oberlender, Rappaport, Bader, Eibenschutz, Wachs from Podgorze, Schleichkorn (baker), Lachs, Liban (producers of lime in Podgorze), Hutter (owners of shops selling musical instruments and bicycles), Horowitz and Frischer (importers of tropical fruits), the well-known family of Landau (Rafal was president of the Jewish community in Cracow), Halpern (a furrier on Grodzka Street), Aleksandrowicz, Wasserberger, Bluhbaum (Persian carpet store)—all gone. Whole dynasties of rabbis perished.

I particularly remember the family Matzner from Podgorze. They were frequent customers in my pharmacy before the war. I recall the old patriarch Matzner, with his great gray beard and his sage adages. It was he who once said, when the talk turned to mutual help among people, "Bread thrown into the river, though well intended, comes back to the thrower against the stream."

Perhaps the list of names mentioned here in my memoir is too long; for the young Cracowians it may not be too important. It does, however, have historical significance. Their listing serves as memorials for those who were our friends and neighbors, cocreators of our city's material and spiritual culture, its arts and sciences. While being good Jews, they were Polish patriots as well, actively participating in the development of Cracow and the Polish motherland.

If we fulfill our obligations to those who died for the motherland, memorialize their names on monuments, so it is morally right to mention in my memoir the names of those who were imprisoned and murdered. This is only a small segment of those known to me, so I hope that I may be forgiven by those whom I do not list because I did not know them.

The famous synagogue dating from the second half of the 14th century, located at Szeroka Street, was almost totally destroyed. It was one of the oldest buildings in Kazimierz. The Germans looted it completely, taking from its archives priceless Torahs, age-old scrolls, Talmuds, and costly prayer vestments. They stole old brass lamps and candelabra and ripped out decorative wall fixtures. These treasures were at first transported to the ghetto and stored in one of the buildings at Limanowska Street. They also demolished the old building "Bergel." According to the legend, the great Talmudic scholar and Cabalist, rabbi, philosopher, and thinker, Nathan Spira, used to lecture there. Old Jewish cemeteries like the one on Szeroka Street and the one surrounding the very old synagogue "Remu," which, incidentally, was transformed into a store, were desecrated and destroyed. So were black marble tombstones bearing the names of famous philosophers, thinkers, and rabbis, like Bach, Jakubowicz, Isserles, the names of the founders and supporters, were smashed. Also vandalized were old synagogues like the Tall, the Isaac, the Popper, the Kupa, and the temple on Miodowa Street.

The newer cemetery on Miodowa Street was devastated. Here, the tombs and tombstones were overturned and broken, granite and marble monuments were torn out. Large black marble slabs were prepared for export because they were needed for paving the walks leading to the villas of the German dignitaries. Two more remote cemeteries were totally destroyed to make way for the concentration camp to be erected in Plaszow. The cemetery at Jerosolimska Street and the one on Abraham Street were included in the projected area of the camp. At these two graveyards, a macabre sight greeted the passersby. The ground, furrowed by picks and shovels, revealed open graves, with skeletons, skulls, and bones strewn about. The Nazi captors destroyed not only the dignity of human life, but profaned that which in the cultures of all nations and peoples of the world was respected and protected, the sanctity of the graves of the dead.

These examples are irrefutable proof of the depths to which blind hatred and insensitivity can sink.

Special mention confirming the remark that "Germans are also people" should be made about those who, despite the Hitlerite terror, were unafraid of the consequences of their defiant behavior; such as a few directors and production shop managers, particularly the Austrians, who, in all good conscience, endangered their lives by helping Poles and Jews. One such man was the Viennese, Julius Madritsch, director of a garment factory for the Germans in Podgorze. He employed the Jews confined at first in the ghetto and later in the Plaszow camp. Madritsch, aware of the conspiracies, created comfortable conditions for them; he not only supplemented the nutrition of the factory workers, but he also transported truckloads of food to the ghetto. The Jewish population, as reported by Dr. Jachniak, an authority on these matters, called Madritsch the "Guardian Angel" of the ghetto and the Plaszow camp.

Next to the camp in Plaszow—where after the liquidation of the ghetto on March 13, 1943, all the Jews who escaped the deportation gathered—were the so-called Julags. These were the workplaces for the Jews, which were beyond the concentration camp in Plaszow; they were billeted there; had their own police and OD, and did not stray beyond the limits of their shop.

No description of the conditions prevailing in the Cracow ghetto would be complete if I did not mention the plants located outside the ghetto limits employing Jews who worked there daily. There was a Julag in Plaszow, situated below the main camp. In the Julag on the Zablocie near Cracow was the enamel factory managed by Oskar Schindler. Jews there were treated humanely. This site existed until September 4, 1944. The workers were then transferred to the camp in Plaszow from where, on October 15, 1944, during the liquidation of the camp in Plaszow, all the factory-employed Jews and many other were resettled in Brunnlitz near Zwitau in Czechoslovakia (Brnenec Svitav). This camp was still headed by Oskar Schindler, who saved it from annihilation.

Another Julag was in Prokocim, where the leader of the OD was my former colleague from the Gymnasium, Lipschutz, an honest man. He was liked by SS Rottenführer Ritschek, to whom he was subordinate and who "patronized" him.

Once Lipschutz excitedly burst into the pharmacy and spoke quickly and in a low voice, "Tadek—today I bet everything on one card—win or lose. I am escaping the camp. I will succeed. You'll see! I will let you know how it went." "Good luck," I said to him, and that last handshake was our final good-bye.

A minute later Ritschek ran into the pharmacy, took Lipschutz with him, and drove back to Prokocim. The next day it was rumored that Lipschutz was shot during his flight.

Julags were still located at the Cracow airport and in the Biezanow where Dr. R. Glassner perished. He would often send me notes asking for medicines and news about his daughter. Contact between us was continually maintained until the death of this charming man.

Hard labor in the Plaszow camp

CHAPTER 6

—The City of the Dead— "Cleaning Up" of the Ghetto —The Hangmen of the Ghetto— The Fate of the OD Men —December 1943—

Upon the liquidation of the ghetto, the existence of the pharmacy was no longer necessary. It seemed to me that after two-and-a-half years of life in that place, I was also "resettled" and consigned to the land of the dead, to a small town emptied of its people, where any errant steps in the desolated streets was a matter of grave concern. When you met a man, you had to shudder. Emptiness was everywhere in those streets, where only a few short hours ago crowds filled the entire area, and smothered the once-filled houses. The specter of death walked the streets, exacting its toll from each building and apartment. No house or room in the former ghetto was exempt from the monstrous crimes. Forlornly I walked through this dead little town, through its empty streets, after two days of my enforced presence in the pharmacy, listening to the echo of my own steps. There must have been many people besides myself who witnessed the most macabre scenes and lived through the horrendous experiences, but I don't think there were too many who felt as I did on that day, immediately after the deportation, walking through the lifeless, bloody, corpse-strewn streets of the destroyed ghetto.

It was dark when I returned to the pharmacy, and the darkness lent an eerie strangeness to the surroundings. From the cloudless sky, the moon cast its silvery gleam on the buildings. The empty streets and squares I passed on my way back seemed even more desolate. Each gate that was ajar, each open window aroused anxiety. As I went by, I heard, or imagined I did, the sound of a window closing. Someone ran quickly through the hall, apparently frightened by my steps, lit a match in the window, and opened it again; suddenly I heard a whistle . . . and a note fluttered down, mysteriously. No—this was no hallucination! This was real! Someone still lived in the building filled with the murdered, hiding in fear of other men who were no different than himself. I picked up the note and quickened my steps. The scenes and experiences, which were still vivid in my mind, precluded a calm consideration of its contents, the meaning of the whispers, remembrance of the places from whence mysterious sounds arose. On my way back to the pharmacy, I met only one person, an OD man, a colleague from my school days, Rottersman, a good and honest man. We greeted each other in silence, not a single word was spoken. Before I entered the pharmacy, I again heard the sound of steps and a knock on the glass. I ran to the gate. There was silence. In the hall, I stumbled over the body of a nude man. I sighed with relief when I reached home in the pharmacy. I looked out of the window on the square, to contemplate the reality of what had happened.

Plac Zgody seemed very strange that night, reminding me of a fairy tale about a bewitched little town. In the light of the moon, the posts and the barbed wire stretched between them formed shadows of innumerable rectangles on the asphalt. The gates of the houses were open, the windows dark. No light—no trace of life. Only dogs running madly about, hiding under the walls of buildings. It was very difficult to fall asleep that night. The emptiness and silence made me nervous; I still had illusions about hearing some footsteps, doors creaking, or knocking on the windows. For many days later when I went out in the ghetto late at night, I seemed to hear these noises. I knew then that they were real. People were sending signals of their survival—they needed help.

Flyers floated down proclaiming, "We are asking for help; please advise someone that we are alive and hungry." But receiving help was not a simple matter. Each stop before an empty building, each careless entry or communication with those in hiding was easily detectable by the German police guards or the sometimes too eager, Jewish OD men. There were not many of the latter who could be trusted. The Germans suspected everyone of being thieves who were concealing Jewish riches that belonged to the SS.

Help, however, was urgent. I chose for this purpose two OD men who were well known to me, Rottersman and Gruner. I told them exactly where I heard voices. I showed them where the slips of paper calling for help fell; we did whatever we could. Several children were smuggled in to the barracks in Plaszow during the transportation of furniture from the epidemic hospital and from the one on Jozefinska Street. The adults in hiding joined groups from the barracks who came to establish order in the ghetto, and together they returned to Plaszow. At first this escaped the attention of the Germans because the number of those returning was not checked too carefully. Later, after several successful escapes from the work groups, it became much more difficult.

Soon after the liquidation of the ghetto, I began to open the pharmacy at ten in the morning, and then only for a few hours daily. Jews working in the ghetto could take advantage of this only during the noontime lunch hour. There were very few who treated themselves medically.

On the first Sunday after the liquidation of the ghetto, I sat in the closed pharmacy reading a book. There was an eerie stillness in the streets. Suddenly I heard a noise. Someone was sneaking in. I listened—a light knock on the door and the sound of rapidly retreating steps. I felt strangely ill at ease. A moment later I heard a tap on the window facing the courtyard. I came nearer and saw the shadow of a man running and then . . . once more, light steps in the hall. I opened the door. Before me was a small boy. "Sir—please help us." "Who are you, where are you hiding?" I asked.

On the boy's haggard, dirty face, I could detect fear and visible evidence of his recent horror. His name was Teufel; his father, before the war, owned a stationery store on Szewska Street. In the ghetto he worked in the paper products contingent and on the 13th of March he was sent, with the others, to the barracks in Plaszow. The boy, together with his aunt and her young baby, remained in the ghetto in a basement hideout under the coal. They had not eaten for several days; the woman was very sick, and the child was dying. They suffered through some terrible moments. Several times Germans passed near them—they trembled, fearing exposure when the child cried—somehow, they survived. They begged for help. I gave them my food, promising to let the father know about their existence. And so I did. A few days later, the aunt joined a group of workers and reached the barracks. The boy managed to get to Plaszow hidden in a hospital closet during the transportation of the inventory. Unfortunately, the baby died.

Time passed quickly. In the dead city, the beginnings of new life were stirring. The ghetto acquired new German supervisors to execute the planned safeguarding and utilization of Jewish property. Such figures as Unterscharführer Hering, SS Rottenführer W. Ritschek, Rottenführer Zugsberger, and Untersturmführer Balb appeared.

Each morning people from the Plaszow barracks arrived. This was the so-called *Säuberungskolonne* (clean-up squad), which was under the direction of the Kapo. They were escorted by Ukrainians in black uniforms and were therefore called "Blacks." After work they returned to the camp. With increasing frequency, I had night visitors who were in hiding, sick or hungry, all asking for help. They came singly and in pairs, some with children.

The clean-up of the ghetto started with the apartment houses near the main square of Podgorze. Sorted-out Jewish possessions were placed in specifically selected buildings. Special workshops were set up to repair and renew furniture right in the place. A locksmith shop was established in order to do repair work and occasional jobs under German orders. In spite of the attempts of the chief of the Plaszow camp, Goeth, to centralize all of the warehousing and installations there, some shops managed to remain in the old ghetto. Many Germans tried by all available means to keep these facilities from being transferred to the camp, because they were afraid that they would then lose their jobs and would be ordered to the front. In addition, large private enterprises were in operation. They supplied some military materiel. They were the firms of Julius Madritsch, in the main square at Podgorze; Zentrale für Handwerkslieferungen located in the building of the old chocolate factory; Optima, on Wegierska Street; tailor and knitting shops, as well as shoemakers, a tannery, a harness and a carpenter shop; also the Wachs lamp factory on Lwowska Street, which manufactured fans for bunker ventilation, ovens for the front and kerosene lamps. In time all of these were transferred to Plaszow. Outside of the ghetto area, the SS established two huge warehouses for furniture and medical and dental equipment. One of these occupied two buildings on Wegierska and Limanowska Streets, in the main square of Podgorze; the second in the large building of the former elementary school at Wielicka Street, where large quantities of books were accumulated. Into these stores were also brought the stolen material from other localities of the so-called Cracow District. Periodically, heavy trucks arrived at these buildings from where the Germans dispatched the furniture and medical items, principally to the Reich for the bombed German population.

The existence of the warehouses outside the ghetto area presented an opportunity for escape. A good number of Jews from the Plaszow camp, assigned to clean the ghetto, took advantage of the guards' laxity and fled. Occasionally, German policemen would help in these ventures, of course for considerable compensation. The Viennese Esel and Schubert and the Volksdeutsch Wita cooperated. The blue police also helped, since their station, bordering on the ghetto, created favorable conditions for escape.

The ghetto clean-up crew worked from six in the morning until six o'clock at night. After that hour, silence enveloped the streets. Only the steps of the

Jewish OD men were sometimes heard. Frequently, SS Rottenführer Ritschek would appear like a ghost, walking or riding a bicycle and accompanied by his ever-present dog Rolf. Kunde and Olde were constant visitors in the ghetto.

Still encircled by barbed wire, the ghetto was guarded night and day by blue and German police guards. It was very difficult to enter, even for high-ranking Germans. Special permission issued by the SSU Polizeiführer in the Oleanders was required. This tight security was ordered because the officers of the SS and SD who came to the ghetto, were stealing goods from the warehouses. These included carpets, paintings, fabrics, and porcelains. The Gestapo and SS men working in the ghetto jealously watched as the results of their efforts were collected by their colleagues. Properly documented reports went to the higher authorities, and the SS issued a regulation which forbade any German to enter or to move about in the ghetto, even those with permission to obtain the requested items. He had to wait to receive these items in the building on Limanowska Street, the backyard of which was in the ghetto. Only those Germans and their wives who were directly connected with the ghetto could enter without special permission. The wives of Oberführer Scherner, Haase, and others visited frequently.

One morning, the clean-up squads came into the ghetto in strange looking clothing. Upon Goeth's order, stripes and squares were painted on their clothes. This was supposed to make their escape more difficult. They looked like circus clowns. At first glance it appeared comical, but the sight did fill with sorrow those whose feelings of human dignity the Germans had not destroyed. I spoke with many people who were not amused by these outlandish uniforms; on the contrary, they evoked feelings of disgust and revulsion for the Germans. The Jews would deride and make jokes about their costumes. Even during their worst moments, many did not lose their innate sense of humor. One of my acquaintances in the painted-stripe suit entered the pharmacy, bowed low, removed his hat with a courtly flourish, and said, "Ladies and gentlemen—I have the honor of informing you that the circus has arrived and the tents are set up in Plaszow. Tickets are not necessary; just approach the gate to gain entry—unfortunately, trying to exit will be more difficult. Frankly I do not advise it."

I remember one of my friends telling me that day, "I am not bothered by it, I am more amused than they could imagine, and there will come a time when the Americans will pay a great deal of money for such a suit and perhaps show it at home as a curiosity of the 20th century."

The clearing of the ghetto was done systematically. The workers in Plaszow were divided into groups which sorted furniture and items made of iron, silver, or copper. Bedrooms were to be stored separately, as well as tables and kitchen equipment. Suitable damaged articles that were repairable were sent to the proper workshops; items in poor condition were thrown into the square on Targowa Street, as were useless old iron pieces. Circling around the workers with a horsewhip in his hand was Rottenführer Ritschek. He was young, a Sudeten German, barely 24 years old, sickly, the son of a third-rate singer, a habitual drunkard, neurotic, and a homosexual. He was a megalomaniac, obsessed with the importance of his mission. He fanatically believed in an ultimate German victory and amused himself by beating the workers and stealing everything from them during his frequent searches. He subscribed to the German dictum that a Jew and his possessions belonged to the SS and that any German could do whatever he wanted to any Jew. He abused people by overworking them, imposed immediate punishment, and threatened them with shooting. He considered himself an idealist, making personal sacrifices and worked dispassionately for no personal gain. He constantly rebuked his colleagues for their seemingly limitless looting of the stores in the ghetto. He was really as corrupt as any of them and always demanded bribes and gifts. All day long he would look for new ways to amuse himself, and at night, dressed in civilian clothes, he roamed the streets of the ghetto looking for a Pole trying to break in. He would lay in wait in the attics for hours on end in buildings in which he suspected looting was taking place. Many denunciations of the Jews still living in the ghetto were attributed to him. His big "achievement" was the discovery of an escape attempt by some of the OD men.

Toward me and my personnel, he behaved correctly, even defending me before the high-ranking SS men Mayer and Balb who, some weeks before the removal of the barbed wire from around the ghetto, wanted to close my pharmacy. A few days before the last Soviet offensive, he appeared in my establishment, having driven from Jaslo, and demanded 4,000 zlotys, threatening to commit suicide in my room if I refused. He maintained that the money from the army safe was lost and if he could not account for its disappearance by a given time, he would be arrested. It was a matter of "honor," etc. I gave him the money because I feared that he was capable of creating some serious problems for me.

About two weeks after the liquidation of the ghetto, all the members of the Judenrat who were still living in the ghetto were seized by order of the SS. As recommended by Goeth, these included Gutter, Streimer, and the members of the OD, Spira, Pacanower, and Susser. They were transported to the camp in Plaszow. Simultaneously, all the Jews who were in the Gestapo service and lived in the city were arrested. The following informers were sent to Plaszow—Gruner, Diamant, Apl, and Förster, among others. There seemed to be some kind of intramural struggle between the SS and the Gestapo. Those arrested who worked for the Gestapo were handled by the SS. In spite of the many antagonisms between the SS and the Gestapo, the two groups were in complete accord on one issue—the murdering of Jews. This particular case, however, concerned individuals who were selected by the Gestapo from among thousands and were used by them for their own purposes. The Gestapo, on the other hand, was abusing the Jews who were "patronized" by the SS. For instance, on a number of occasions they arrested Chilowicz, director of the Jewish camp militia in Plaszow. Since he was trusted by Goeth, they hoped that these seizures would upset Goeth and manifest their authority. This, of course, forced Goeth to intervene quite frequently, which in turn would result in stormy sessions.

After arriving at Plaszow, those arrested were herded into one barrack. Goeth appeared soon, beating many unmercifully and then announcing that they would be shot. When the Gestapo learned this, they decided to release them. The incident caused a furor, but the prisoners were finally released. Several weeks later, the members of the Judenrat, Gutter and Streimer, were shot along with their families. I remember the dispute between Goeth and Kunde, because Kunde arrested Chilowicz. The argument was settled by Haase, who was Goeth's superior. He sided with and protected Kunde. Haase ordered Goeth to come to the OD in the ghetto, and there was a rather sharp exchange of words. This was overheard by the OD men and they related it to me a few minutes after it happened. During the argument —which, by the way, was quite loud—Kunde stung Goeth. "You might outrank me, but there is this difference between us—I can arrest you at any moment on the authority of this shield," and he pulled from his pocket a police badge on a chain. "And if you really wanted to do this to me, you would have obtained an order for my arrest from your superiors." The discussion ended then with Kunde's victory and Haase's sharp rebuke of Goeth.

The Germans brought their own work to the repair shop where the Jews were employed. The locksmith shops located on Targowa Street and later on Jozefinska Street were, for the most part, busy opening safes found in the Jewish apartments, usually empty, and then repairing them. They also produced, on special orders of the SS men, artistic lamps under the experienced eyes of the experts Adolf Giemski and Silberstein. Iron doors for the villas of Scherner and Haase; iron fences, manacles, etc., were also fabricated.

On orders from Scherner, three lamps were hand-forged with decorations in this shop. For ornamentation they designed thick rings, which linked the spreading arms of the lamp. Before these rings were mounted, a list of all the crimes of Scherner and Haase were engraved in Hebrew on the inner surface. I received the third one of these lamps as a gift, but without the engravings.

There was quite a famous affair involving Majer Goldstein, a ghetto dweller, who left it and remained in Cracow with Aryan papers. One day, betrayed by the informer Cabaja (a Gypsy), he was arrested and brought to the ghetto for interrogation. During the inquiry, he confessed that he knew of a place outside Cracow where dollars and gold items were buried. A Gestapo agent accompanied Goldstein to Opatkowice because there had been some talk about this place. There Goldstein found the spot where the treasures were supposedly buried and started to dig. At an opportune moment, he slammed the shovel down on the Gestapo man's head, who fell to the ground bleeding. Goldstein ran and hid in a nearby thicket. He remained there until nighttime and then, in darkness, ran as far as possible.

In the empty ghetto—until the time of the removal of the barbed wire in September of 1943, the building of the OD was occupied by a police division, the SS, and the Gestapo. A prison was there, too, and offices where the Gestapo interrogated Jews who were caught with Aryan papers or were denounced by informers. There, records of the evacuation of the ghetto were filed. There, too, originated the reports about the mood of Polish society; also included were the communications of informers about concealed people and information on the whereabouts of hidden valuables left by the Jews. Prisoners were occasionally dispatched from there to Plaszow, marked for death or for labor. Kunde officiated continually here, and Olde was visited often by Frommer. The prison warden was the OD man Gruner; the hospital physician was the fine doctor, Armer. The prison resembled a chicken coop, completely surrounded by barbed wire and brightly illuminated by reflectors. In the courtyard, the roll calls and lineups were conducted. In spite of the vigilance of the guards, several bold and successful escapes were achieved.

Kunde visited me almost everyday. On his way through Plac Zgody, he would drop in and ask me what was new in politics since yesterday; what do the Poles talk about among themselves? He asked me to be completely open with him and said I should not regard him as a German in uniform but as a human being. He assured me about his positive attitude towards the Poles and uttered rather risky criticisms of the government, of Frank and Scherner; he was furious about the government directives and signs "FOR GERMANS ONLY." He explained this to me in an indirect manner: Germans don't consider the Poles as "Untermenschen," as the propaganda would have it. It is well known, however, that a Pole in close contact with a German is able to trap him into committing transgressions inimical to his own country. It would be unthinkable in the Reich for transgressions such as the disappearance of carloads of food, coal, and alcohol, taking bribes, listening to foreign broadcasts, or betraying State secrets and details of arrests and other actions to occur. Cursing the war, Kunde called the German politicians "idiots at green tables." He blamed the conflict on the American and English Jews. He was very proud of the result of his work as Kriminalsekretär. He explained to his superiors that he was so successful because, "I never beat anybody, I don't shout, I speak calmly if I can, I promise that those arrested will go to work in the camp and not be executed . . . but I always keep my promises, and that is the reason for my successes." I took a chance and told him what I thought every Pole said and felt about Germany at that time. I assured Kunde that we were all certain that the Germans would lose the war, that we would regain our independence, and that none of us believed that the Anglo-Saxons would take up arms against Russia as the Germans thought and hoped they would. I talked with him about the arrests of Polish scientists and their incarceration in camps where many lost their lives, about the constant raids in the streets and cafés, about the dire extremes to which this system had driven the Poles. He sometimes nodded in agreement, but blamed the leaders.

He realized what would happen in the event of a German defeat and contemplated—as he half-jokingly put it—the idea of escaping abroad. On each furlough he would travel to the Reich with foreboding thoughts, and on his return he would report to me about the prevailing mood there. He told me about the colossal destruction caused by the bombings. He confessed that during his stay in Germany he tried to convince his colleagues of the hopelessness of their situation, explaining that defeat, in his opinion, was inevitable. He would receive assurances from his colleagues about a secret new weapon which they would use shortly. He gave me all the details about it "because a friend of his was employed on its production." This awesome force would destroy vegetation and all life, and result in the earth's permanent infertility for a radius of many kilometers. This news rekindled Kunde's faith in a German victory. He shared this belief with me, but I had the distinct impression that in the General Government these stories were not widely believed. I then told him that we had also heard about this weapon, but that we were generally dubious about its effectiveness, and it was rumored that it was being used to bolster the morale of their people. If the

Germans really had such powerful munitions, would it not be most propitious to use it now? What were they waiting for?

Quite often I wanted to take advantage of my acquaintance with Kunde to help the imprisoned Poles. I remember that I was asked to intervene in the arrest of Dr. Jan Regula, assistant secretary of the Jagellonian University. Kunde refused my plea in his behalf, informing me that he wanted to be honest and did not like to delude me with false hope. He could not intercede because it was under the jurisdiction of a department with which he did not work directly. Any intervention would certainly arouse suspicion. He could handle any case that fell within the purview of his own department and if the problem was not too complicated. Several times, when it came to Jews he proved to me that he could fulfill his promises. After the liquidation of the ghetto, older people were occasionally transferred from the overcrowded prison to Plaszow where, as a rule, they were shot unless, as seldom happened, the documents indicated that they were to be kept alive. On two occasions I interceded with Kunde, at the last moment, in behalf of elderly women; he promised that they would not be shot and he kept his word. Kunde was frequently sympathetic to the pleading of the ladies in my employ and saved the lives of acquaintances who were sent from the prison to the Plaszow camp.

The relationships among Germans in the ghetto—as far as could be observed—were infused with pronounced distrust. There was no confiding, and they were fearful and cautious. Of course, in the company of one another they were very polite, and they lavishly praised their superiors. They never criticized the decisions and activities of high-ranking officers. They were also firmly convinced that Germany would be victorious. But should any one of them fall from grace, they would be roundly insulted, cursed, and called "thief" and "coward." I remember how, after Scherner and Haase were arrested for cheating and thievery, their subalterns were overcome with joy. This was the time when all kinds of stories about the private lives of those who were arrested surfaced. I asked what would happen with Scherner and Haase, and voiced my opinion that they would be sent to the front. "Fighting alongside a thief would offend and dishonor the German soldier. The best that they could expect would be their inglorious return to civilian life." This was their answer. The charges against Haase, among others, was that he unlawfully appropriated paintings including one by Wojciech Kossak. It should be added that Kossak's paintings were particular favorites of the Germans; so, of course, it was a major offense. Where did he get it? Haase said that he obtained it from Kunde in the ghetto.

Kunde was therefore interrogated, but he denied all the charges and he named as the source the Jewish informers, Steinfeld and Brodman, who were in the service of the Gestapo and customs control post. Since Haase, behind bars, would not be dangerous, and Kunde maintained all of his power, Steinfeld corroborated Kunde's testimony that it was they who gave him the painting on orders from Haase.

Kunde was saying, "Today one has to be very careful because envy knows no limit. I knew a colleague who, in a position similar to mine, occasionally deposited money in the bank in such large sums that it came to the attention of the authorities. When he could not satisfactorily reveal the sources of this income, he was jailed." Kunde continued, "To avoid any trace of suspicion, I do not wear rings, I own a steel watch, I don't have a silver cigarette case, I do not frequent bars, and don't go to theaters—to avoid calling attention to myself. If I want to entertain, I do it at home only."

He expressed himself in superlatives about the OD men, Spira, Pacanower, and Susser. He once explained why such a simpleton like Spira was elevated to the job of manager of the OD. "The selection was made for psychological reasons. If this position were filled by an intelligent, well-educated man, coming from a different social strata, he would be lost and completely out of place. Instead of working closely with us, he would only make our job more difficult. That was the case with Dr. Rosenzweig. He was not a dependable man; he did not care to and could not work like Spira or Gutter." These two could be bought with a new fancy uniform, which made them feel superior to the others. Although they could leave the ghetto at any time, they wouldn't even entertain the idea of running away. The feeling of power that accompanied rank had to be developed within them. That's why the authorities were incensed at SS Pilarzik for slapping Spira in the face. Pilarzik received a reprimand, and Spira knew this. It bolstered his faith in his own power. He worked eagerly, probably until the very end. Spira's interventions were usually successful. People close to Spira were usually released when arrested, were pulled out of transports to assure him of his special rights. This was his reward for his faithful service. In the end he found out at the price of his own life that these favors were a sham.

Only once did I have anything to do with Spira and I went to see him in the OD. I wanted to take advantage of Kunde's absence to visit the Kessler family who were imprisoned there. The Kessler family, baptized long ago, was comprised of Dr. of Law Maximillian Kessler, who was director of the Commercial Bank in Cracow; his wife and daughter, who graduated from the highly regarded Gymnasium of the Ursuline Sisters, and a son. And imagine—Kessler stayed on at his job until 1943 and his entire family moved about the city freely and fearlessly. Then suddenly came the startling news. The Gestapo arrested the whole family, sealed the apartment and transported them to the ghetto. I was asked to collect scribbled notes and to impart news to the prisoners, and, what was most important, to plead with Kunde for the lives of the Kesslers from an imminent sentence, which threatened all of the ghetto prisoners.

For the present, I did not want to ask Kunde for permission to speak with the Kesslers because I could not very well tell him the reason I was so interested in speaking with them. I therefore approached Spira, who emphatically refused. He was very sorry but he would not betray Kunde's trust for anything. "This is unthinkable," he said. The decisiveness of his refusal left me no alternative but to contact Kunde directly. After brief consideration, Kunde said that he was really not opposed to granting my request, but what would Spira and his associates think about it? It would appear strange and he could expect some dissension from them.

"You know what," he said. "You go to Spira alone when I am not around and ask him. He will certainly not refuse you."

I confessed that I had already done this but got nowhere because Spira turned me down in no uncertain terms. Kunde smiled with satisfaction: "I am surprised that he refused, but I admire his discipline. Yes, this is a man one can depend upon. I will allow you a visit," he said, after a while.

And indeed, I made several such visits. Later I pleaded with Kunde not to send Kessler to Plaszow where death awaited him at the hands of Goeth. I explained that I had known the family for many years, that the director had once arranged a loan for me from the bank, and that this money saved me at the time. I personally was very grateful to him for his help.

Kunde listened, looked into my eyes, and remained silent for a long time. Finally, he changed the subject. Many days passed, and although he visited me at the pharmacy daily, this topic was never mentioned again by me or by Kunde. One day, however, Kunde did ask me whether someone had interceded with me in behalf of Kessler. I answered "No," and repeated that only I had asked, and now once again I was earnestly beseeching. Again, not a word from Kunde. Knowing Kunde well, I was gaining confidence: certainly, if he were able—and I was sure that he was—he would not be indifferent. But I realized that I would have to be patient and not belabor the subject.

Several weeks passed, and I was running out of time. Kunde still remained silent. The Kesslers, despairing behind prison bars, waited anxiously each day for some news. Unfortunately, I couldn't bring them any hopeful assurances of safety.

One afternoon Kunde visited the pharmacy. With quick steps, he entered my duty room, sat down, and looking coldly at me asked, "What will happen to the Kesslers?" I wondered what he meant by this question. He was asking me instead of the other way round! What could I answer? I repeated my plea for the third time, but I quickly thought: something must be happening; Kunde's question gave me a bit of hope; he had not forgotten—he was thinking about the fate of the Kesslers. A moment of silence—he glanced downward at my face, stood up, said goodbye, and left. A few days later he came in again and asked me to accompany him to my duty room. After closing the doors of the other rooms, he said in a lowered voice: "You have to take care of a certain problem for me, as quickly as possible. You must find a Polish doctor who will perform an abortion on a certain woman who, he will be told, is your girlfriend. You realize of course that this is a very delicate matter, particularly since this lady is German. The rest is up to you; I must not be involved in this affair; it must be kept secret, and I am sure that I don't have to remind you what would happen if anyone else found out about it."

I was sure that no Polish doctor would do this, and I certainly did not want to be known as the errant lover of a German woman. I thought of a plan, which I suggested to Kunde: From the camp in Plaszow, under the pretext of interrogation, he should bring out Dr. Regina Feniger, a highly esteemed gynecologist, and a Mrs. Erwina Order-Panzer, a nurse who worked in the Gynecology Department in the ghetto hospital and later in the poor excuse for a hospital in the camp, and a third person as a decoy so that Goeth should not get suspicious. The procedure would be performed in the duty room of the pharmacy, perhaps with assistance of Dr. W. Armer who would administer the anaesthesia, and me.

Kunde agreed and decided on the date. My plan succeeded. In the afternoon at about one o'clock, he brought in his lady and then quickly disappeared with a promise to stop by in the evening. At three o'clock everyone was in place. Just before the operation, I informed Dr. Feniger about the entire business. She said that she had somehow guessed what it was all about when she was told that together with Mrs. Order she was to go to the post where Kunde and Olde officiated.

Everything went well. The ladies who were brought in from Plaszow left together with the third person whom Kunde had included, ostensibly for interrogation. Later it was discovered that this was a young woman who was caught with Aryan papers in Cracow and sent to Goeth for his disposition. There was no doubt about her fortunate fate. Kunde, happy about the way things turned out, informed Goeth that this person would be needed again in his investigation, and she should therefore not be deported. In this way, we were able to save a young life. Fortunately, she survived the war. Both my lady coworkers were in the attic waiting for the completion of the operation. That night, Kunde came for his lover. He arrived on a bicycle. The robust wench leaped nimbly from the couch and accompanied her beloved to the ghetto gate, where a taxi was waiting for them. Kunde bid me good-bye and said in parting, "I will never forget you for this." When they departed, I was freed from the heavy burden of responsibility for the whole episode. My ladies left the attic and we started a thorough clean-up.

Goeth was informed that both women, Dr. Regina Feniger and Mrs. Order, would continue to be at the disposition of Kunde.

Susser, secretary of the OD, was the only one who had a terrible premonition of their future. He would constantly repeat with maniacal stubbornness: "They will finish us all." He was particularly obstinate in this regard when the OD men were forbidden to live outside the ghetto—in spite of the fact that they were given Argentine papers by the Gestapo and permission to rent apartments in the city. When they did find an apartment, they encountered delays in leaving the ghetto. They were persuaded, in a friendly fashion to live together as long as a prison existed.

One of the OD workers was Dr. Armer, who joined that organization in the last days of the ghetto, wishing to postpone his departure for Plaszow. He and his wife and daughter had Hungarian papers. I was outside of the ghetto when he received these. Later, it was learned that the foreign documents were ingeniously forged by members of the RPZ (Council for Jewish Help). The forgers were Wladyslaw Wichman, using the alias of "Wladyslaw," former director of the school in Podgorze, Edward Kubiczek, painter and engraver, and Zozislaw Kasperek, who supplied the photos. A continual contact was maintained with them through Ferdynand Arczynski, a member of the RPZ in Warsaw, who frequently visited Cracow.

Capitalizing on the good mood of Kunde and in consideration of the successful operation in which Dr. Armer played a leading role, I risked asking whether he could obtain validation of Armer's Hungarian papers. Kunde, somewhat surprised, stared at me and after a moment of silence asked, "Where are these papers?" "I have them with me," I replied and handed them over to him. He studied them for a long time, put them in his pocket, and said that he would bring them back the next day.

He did indeed keep his word. As he gave me the authorized papers, he whispered, "Sagen Sie ihm, er soll sofort verschwinden." (Tell him that he should disappear immediately).

A few days later when he met Dr. Armer in the pharmacy, he repeated his advice and left. Armer could not decide about leaving the ghetto and he kept delaying their departure until the final liquidation of the members of the OD and the prisoners under arrest. He was executed in the Plaszow camp together with his wife and daughter.

One day, there was a great hubbub in the ghetto. Two of the OD men, who registered several months before as possessors of visas to America, were called by Kunde to the OD and were told that they could use these documents. After passing quarantine, they could use public transportation to one of the ports in northern Germany. There was a great deal of joy among them. It seemed almost unbelievable that after years of unbearable hell, they would again become free people; they would be able to reclaim their possessions, remove their Jewish armbands and leave the country! They were ordered to report the next day to the so-called Helcel in the old people's home, and from there, after passing through quarantine, they could leave. These men were Ing. Ringel and Kerner. One had a wife, another a wife and a baby. All were ecstatic about their good luck and they were envied. They drank a good deal that day. The pharmacy, deprived of regular business for many months, was converted into a delicatessen selling liquors, sausages, and cookies. Just as in some American stores with liquor licenses, one could eat and drink as much as one wished, from 190 proof whiskies to liqueurs to suit any taste. People drank every day, sometimes more than once. On that day, however, almost the entire ghetto was tipsy. The following day, these decent people were tearfully saying good-bye. They left by a horse-drawn cab, loaded down with their possessions. After their departure, they were never heard from again. Once, a card was received from Ringel on his way to Hanover; later, it was rumored that he died suddenly, and mystery surrounded their ultimate fate. No one heard anything further about Kerner.

Some time later, another incident occurred in the ghetto. Ritschek's adjutant was the OD man Weitz, a German Jew who was his trusted consultant, and Ritschek really liked him. Weitz had a very sick wife, a schizophrenic who displayed suicidal tendencies. On several occasions she tried to poison herself with Luminal, but she was saved each time. She was a daily visitor at the pharmacy for purchases of pills. She would tell us that she was sure to meet her end as a suicide. "This is no life," she would say. "I die every day; it is not really true that you die only once. All that is happening to and around us is so cruel that living under these conditions for long is impossible."

Once, Weitz quarreled with Chilowicz, who was a protégé of Goeth. This fight took place on Limanowska Street near the building where the furniture was stored. During that encounter Chilowicz, apparently insulted by a disrespectful remark by Weitz, slapped his face and threatened to report him to Goeth. This was terrible, because Goeth's reactions were well known. Weitz, who was a psychopath, was so worried that he committed suicide that night. Ritschek was furious and threatened to shoot Chilowicz. He carried out Wietz's body. The ghetto was stunned by Ritschek's behavior.

Once, Weitz accused me before Ritschek of storing Jewish possessions. He said that liquor was sold in the pharmacy, and that I was an intermediary in transferring mail between Jews who worked in the ghetto and their Polish acquaintances on the other side of the Vistula. Ritschek confided this to Kunde who categorically denied it. Nevertheless, he told me about it and warned me that there could be a search of my pharmacy and the apartments of my lady coworkers.

"You are lucky that this happened with me here, because otherwise it could be quite dangerous," he said.

I thanked him with gifts of a bottle of vodka and a box of cigars. This sealed the fortunate solution of the problem. It was not the first time that Kunde had saved my life.

The routine of daily work in the ghetto was occasionally interrupted by the dignitaries of the SS, Haase and Mayer. The presence of Haase in the streets engendered a nervousness of lesser severity than did the more infrequent visits of Goeth, which instilled fear and terror. The ghetto would dig in at such times by hiding in the buildings and workshops. No one dared appear in the streets then.

The prolongation of the stay in the ghetto of my personnel and me subjected us to a required renewal of our passes every fourteen days. Kunde would attend to this.

Once, shortly before the barbed wire around the ghetto was removed, I was visited by Sturmbannführer Mayer and Untersturmführer Balb. They were amazed. "An Aryan, who is a Pole—what is he doing here? Pharmacy—what for? For whom?" they asked. After a cursory inspection of the room itself, they examined the drawers, then decided that tomorrow I would have to close the pharmacy. They explained that, after all, Jews were forbidden to have money, so, to whom did I sell? Ritschek defended me, noting that I also sent medications to the camp because the distribution section of the

Jewish Social Self-Help were without them. They left, but not convinced that my shop was needed. I was quite disturbed after their departure. This would be most unfortunate, I thought, to exist all this time in the ghetto, to survive all the deportations, and then just before the very end, to be closed down. This was the worst kind of luck!

Half an hour passed—Kunde came in. I told him about the visitors I had and of their directive. Kunde asked me whether I showed them my papers, and whether they had read them. "Of course," I replied. Without a word, he sat down at the typewriter and prepared the passes for us, but not for a two week period as before, but for a month. He wanted to let me know in this way, that he could do a lot if he wanted. He told me that he argued "in the OD there was a jail in which a number of foreigners were held, many of whom were sick—a pharmacy was therefore vital. It also supplied Weichert with medicines and filled prescriptions for the camp's inhabitants."

In addition to Kunde, his assistant Olde often visited me in the pharmacy. In spite of the friendship between the two, when Olde appeared, the conversation would turn from politics to other subjects. Olde, who was about 43 years of age, was one of the few Germans who spoke quietly and calmly. He was born in Hamburg, was married and the father of two children. He always studiously avoided political discussions. Occasionally, Commander Bousko would drop into the pharmacy. He disliked all of them. He used to say that they were undependable and insincere.

And so the days passed. One after another, the apartment buildings were emptied. The deserted ghetto was unreal, as if the final hour was imminent. Ritschek and Zugsberger fumed, screamed all day long, and beat the workers. Tired Jews carried heavy loads on their backs, transferring furniture from one warehouse to another, unloading material from other ghettos, stacking it in designated buildings which were transformed into permanent warehouses. There were specific buildings for the storage of stationery, leather, lingerie, textiles, and the like. People working in the ghetto would eat here, in the communal kitchen. The food was obtained by collecting provisions left behind in the apartments by those who were consigned to the camp.

Each day, horse-drawn flat trucks driven by Poles would appear in the ghetto to transport furniture outside the boundaries of the quarter. The contents of the trucks were stored in the building on Limanowska Street. Sometimes the furniture was delivered directly to German apartments. The furnishings of the arrested Jews who were hiding in the city were confiscated and taken to the ghetto. Everything was tradeable. Through buying, selling, and exchanging, everything was disposed of. Ritschek was frequently absent during these transactions. However, he knew every detail about each deal and the price that was paid—the money went into his pocket.

The nearer the clearing of the former ghetto was completed, the more frequent were the incidents of escapes from the Säuberungskolonne. They fled individually or in groups. Some OD men with foreign papers, working for the Gestapo, took advantage of occasional opportunities and fled across the frontier. Schleifer escaped with his wife and child; later on, so did Neiger and his family, and after them, Turk. This last flight could have serious consequences. The remaining OD men were terribly fearful. Spira went mad and the excitement and anxiety helped to bring on an attack of gallstones. On the following day, Kunde was informed of this situation. He disregarded it and ordered that everything should proceed as if nothing had happened. He was a strange man!

At about that time, two weddings took place in the ghetto at which a rabbi officiated. He reported for work with the clean-up squad by special permission of the SD. Spira, the director of the OD, married off his daughter to an OD man; and one of the managers of the SS warehouses, Demmer, married a young lady from the camp. She joined him to live in the ghetto. These festivities were honored by the presence of Haase, Kunde, and Ritschek. After several weeks the newlywed Demmers, together with the other managers of the warehouses, were transferred to the camp and then executed. After a time, the majority of the OD ghetto crew met the same fate. For several more weeks, the remaining handful of OD men in the ghetto were deluded into thinking that they would be permitted to live with their parents in the city or to cross the border.

The empty buildings betokened utter desolation. In the squares, in the blind alleys, and in the large courtyards, piles of old, useless furniture and stacks of iron rose to the height of a full story. In Plac Zgody, countless peripatetic closets, tables, and credenzas were being ruined. An order was issued to empty a building filled with furniture in the impossible time of two hours. It was accomplished, however, under the personal supervision of Ritschek who, wishing to display his eagerness and expertise, ordered the furniture to be thrown out from the upper floors. Tables, closets, beds were hurled down and splintered noisily on the pavement just to implement a stupid directive. During the emptying of the apartments, the cleaners would occasionally find valuables. With the help of the Poles in the city, they would sell these. Larger items were removed in boxes and loaded onto the platform trucks in the ghetto.

In the first few weeks after the resettling of the Jews in the Plaszow camp, the Germans, through their informers or by chance, discovered hideouts in the ghetto. Groups of Germans and OD men, under the direction of Spira, aided by workmen with axes, picks, and steel bars, moved in. They discovered ingenious hideaways in the attics and basements. Stocked with food and water the hiders could live for months, barring betrayal. Those rounded up were transferred to detention in the OD. They were then sent to Plaszow, usually to their death.

While cleaning the houses, bodies of the victims of poisonings, shootings, exhaustion or diseases, dead for weeks or months, would be found in the basements under mounds of coal. The presence of untold numbers of flies often led to the finding of decomposed bodies. I saw corpses in a state of indescribable decay; I saw the body of a woman lying under a featherbed quite probably for many weeks, or even months. She had died in her own bed on the day of deportation. Maggots had infested and eaten her body, which was beyond recognition. I found a young girl in her bed, possibly poisoned by her parents who were refused permission to take her to the camp. I discovered in a basement the hand of an old man extended upward from under a load of coal. The transportation of the dead and murdered in the ghetto was attended to by a cemetery keeper, a well-known figure in the ghetto, Pinkoza Ladner, nicknamed "Pinie Koza" (Pinie the Goat). He was permitted to live with his wife and child in a tiny accommodation in the Aryan sector in the cemetery building on Miodowa Street. After the liquidation of the ghetto, the Germans killed Pinkoza and his entire family.

In the background of these tragedies, the proverbial faithfulness of the dogs left behind by their masters was movingly accentuated. Deserted by their owners, they roamed the area all day long searching for food. After they found something to eat, they would return to their homes and lie under the beds of their masters. I remember the case of a pinscher, the beloved dog of one of my physician acquaintances. Every day he would come to the apartment of an OD man. The hungry dog would sit for hours in front of the door, but he was not caught. After he ate his food, he would return home and sit under the bed, and would not allow anyone to come near until hunger forced him out again to the apartment of the OD man. Finally, that man managed to catch the pinscher. He kept him for two days, feeding him well. After that time, however, the dog escaped to his own home.

In the evenings, one dog would constantly come to the pharmacy and after a time he brought a friend with him for dinner. We had to coax the animals for a long time to get them to come inside. At the beginning we would bring the food and drink to them in the street. After a while, they did enter the pharmacy, where they ate their portions of food. Immediately after they had finished eating, they would race home. Only one little bulldog became fond of us and remained with us in the pharmacy.

The number of buildings that had not yet been emptied of furniture was growing smaller daily. The area of the ghetto was rapidly decreasing because whole blocks of streets were being continually detached. The warehouses were bulging with stored things. Books gathered from all the apartments and transported from all the ghettos of the Cracow district were accumulated at first in one house on Jozefinska Street, and later in the former school on Wielicka Street. The more valuable German books were seized by the Germans; Polish and Jewish books were sold as scrap for practically nothing. Among the latter were splendid editions of the great Polish poets, excellent literature, trade books, and valuable collections of Hebrew and Jewish works, religious and lay. Prayer books and beautiful leather-bound volumes taken from the synagogues were left in the courtyards, ruined by rain.

We were successful in saving and preserving a number of Torah scrolls and religious volumes. After the Germans left, I turned them over to a state Jewish historical committee on Dluga Street in Cracow. I gave a few small books to some of my Jewish friends. We hid the oldest and most valuable Torahs, chosen by Dr. Armer, an authority, in carefully selected places, transferring them first to the attic, then to the basement, until I found and camouflaged a perfect hiding place located in the front room of the pharmacy. A carpenter from the ghetto put the finishing touches to it.

In this cache, I kept the Torahs, in compliance with the instructions of Dr. Armer, who would say "He who saves a Torah was as blessed as if he had saved a man." Torahs must stand vertically, covered with a satin sheath, and thus they remained until the end of the war.

A few days after I donated the books, I received a letter from the Jewish Historical Committee in Cracow thanking me for our overall behavior in the ghetto. The Torahs, however, were not mentioned. In the recently opened Jewish museum in the old synagogue on Szeroka Street, I could find no trace of them among the other priceless liturgical items.

Hardly a week passed in the ghetto that Jews were not brought in. They were the ones who were caught in the city identifying themselves with Polish papers. The accused were first examined by Dr. Armer, who was supposed to pass judgment regarding circumcision. The arrested men contended that they were operated upon to relieve infection, which left a scar indistinguishable from the ritual surgery. Dr. Armer's finding in each case was that the scar could be the result of circumcision or a health-related operation, and he was therefore not able to state conclusively, based on his examination, whether the man was of Jewish descent.

In the final stage of the clean-up, the ghetto experienced two unusual events: the birthdays of Ritschek, Zugsberger, and most notably that of Kunde. On those occasions the presentation of gifts was profuse. Virtually all the Germans were drunk. They left earlier than usual to attend to festivities in their apartments. They also curbed their beatings of the workers, and they somehow seemed reluctant to otherwise mistreat them.

During the clearing of the apartment houses, Ritschek beat the workers mercilessly, shooting one of them. On one occasion in the OD courtyard when all the workers were assembled, one of them was singled out after certain items he picked up when cleaning the apartments were not reported to the authorities. Sentence was pronounced immediately and executed on the spot. Flogging was often imposed. The guilty would receive twenty-five lashes on the bare back for any transgression. Haase was present when a not so young woman was inhumanly flogged.

All collected items which, in the opinion of the Germans, were no longer useful were immediately sold to the Poles who were crowded around the front of the barbed wire.

In August of 1943, the wire surrounded only the OD building and several neighboring apartment houses. After March 13, 1943, the only Jewish institution in the old ghetto was the building on Jozefinska Street 2A. This structure housed general merchandise and the dispensary of the Jewish Social Self-Help, whose name was changed to JUS (Judische Unterstutzungsstelle). Its director was Dr. Weichert, a lawyer by profession, a man of unusual capabilities, extremely intelligent, an excellent organizer. Before the war, he was one of the foremost representatives of the Jewish cultural world. He had an abiding interest in the dramatic arts, organized and directed the Warsaw experimental theater, and wrote extensively on theatrical arts. During the war, he was the head of the Jewish Social Self-Help in Warsaw. After its activity encompassed the whole of the General Government, he was elected chairman of a seven-man presidium and was transferred with his wife, daughter, and son to Cracow, where they lived in the ghetto. As a ranking functionary of the International Red Cross, gifts for the Jews were received by him.

After March 1943, with the agreement of the German authorities, he moved to the building on Jozefinska Street. There he skillfully organized, jointly with Dr. Hilfstein, Dr. Tisch, Mgr. A. Biberstein, Ing. S. Jaszczurka, and Dr. L. Leinkram, the distribution of medicine and food to the camp in

Plaszow and all the others in Poland. After visiting the camps in Plaszow and all others in Cracow and its surroundings, he helped the inmates, groups or individuals at the risk of his own life. He carried correspondence and monies received from the Poles for the Jews. Correspondence and funds that came into our pharmacy were distributed by him personally. Medicines and food saved many from certain death. Dr. Weichert lived each day never knowing whether he would be liquidated during the night. This uncertainty was bolstered by a persistent rumor about barracks being built for the use of JUS in Plaszow. The RPZ (Jewish Fighting Organization) worked very closely with Dr. Weichert to help Jews in the various camps. This assistance reached beyond the government area. The hostile attitude of Goeth, who hated the Red Cross and civilian authorities' directives regarding Dr. Weichert, was not a good omen for the time when he would eventually be transferred to Plaszow. In July of 1944, during the panicky flight of the German armies from the eastern front, the SS authorities decided to liquidate the JUS post. Informed of this, Dr. Weichert and his family did not sleep at home. The doctor's fears were well founded. One morning, cars carrying SS men arrived to arrest him. His absence from the building of the JUS saved him from certain death.

The Weicherts had the RPZ to thank for saving and hiding them. Its central headquarters were located in Warsaw under the code name "Zegota." It was created in 1942. The founder of the Cracow committee of the RPZ, which was organized in 1943, was Prof. Tadeusz Seweryn (Socha). Participating in the organization for the district of Cracow were representatives of various political parties. Dr. Stanislaw Dobrowolski (code name Staniewski) was elected as chairman; the secretary was Mgr. Wladyslaw Wojcik (code name Zegota), both from the PPS (Polish Socialist Party); the treasurer was Anne Dobrowolski (alias Michalska), Democratic Party. The Jewish Society was represented by the beautiful Mrs. Maria Hochberg, known as Marianska. In addition to these, many other people cooperated, including the mother, sister, and wife of Mgr. Wojcik.

The RPZ president, S. Dobrowolski, hid the Weichert family in the apartment of his sister. Dr. Docent Miklaszewska, who was well known in Cracow, soon after moved the hidden family to the apartment of her friend Mrs. Wanda Dwernicka. She lived in Cracow on Zyblikiewicza Street (today The Battle of Lenin Street). They lived there through the occupation and survived for liberation. During the Weicherts' stay with Mrs. Dwernicka, a strong bond of friendship between the hostess and her guests developed. The wife of Dr. Weichert, Franciszka, a very beautiful and charming woman, along with her daughter and son, selflessly helped her husband with his heavy workload. His job was to prepare medicines to replenish the stocks of many small pharmacies. These were then sent to all the Jewish camps and wherever Jews were billeted. Many people survived because they were able to get the needed medication.

After Poland regained its independence, Dr. Weichert was sued for not obeying the recommendation of the Jewish underground organization to cease his activities. The position of Dr. Weichert and his views in this matter were diametrically opposed to the views of the organization. In the court proceedings he maintained that he wished to remain in contact with the representative of the underground in order to present his position and to prove that he really helped the people interned in the camps. The organization, however, disagreed with his contentions and even issued an order for his liquidation, which did not take place. The trial proved conclusively that Dr. Weichert could, with the help of Polish and Jewish organizations, have gone abroad or hidden in a monastery. But he never availed himself of these opportunities. He proved, without a doubt, that the assistance which he provided saved the lives of many people. A few years after the war, the Weicherts left Poland and settled in Israel where the doctor was heartily welcomed by his former students and friends.

To the very end of his full, rich life, Dr. Weichert occupied himself with cultural and literary matters. He published three volumes of memoirs and a large volume devoted to the Jewish Social Self-Help organization. He died in Tel Aviv in 1967. The fourth volume of his memoirs was published posthumously on his eightieth birthday.

The final act in the destruction of the ghetto was played out during the nights of the 14th to 15th of December 1943. At 7:45 P.M., truckloads of armed SS men arrived in front of the OD building, with Goeth in charge. All the members of the OD were loaded into these vehicles, together with their families, without their belongings. The jailed were also seized. They were transported to the camp in Plaszow, and there they were all executed with the exception of the family of a Hungarian citizen, Mrs. Katz and her children, and Dr. Kessler, his wife, son, and daughter. Many months later, during one of the deportations, the wife and daughter were taken to an extermination camp and perished there. Kessler and his son survived the war and regained their freedom. Kunde kept his promise.

Just a few hours before the last inhabitants of the ghetto were carried away, I was in the OD interceding with Kunde for the Kessler family. Kunde's nervous state made a strong impression on me. He worked in his office from early morning, drank vodka, and constantly kept looking at his watch. After assuring me that he remembered my request, he tried to get me out of the OD building as quickly as possible. He escorted me personally to the gate, asking Dr. Armer to open it.

I said good-bye to Dr. Armer, not suspecting that in a few short hours he would be executed. Bad luck seemed to dog him. He did everything possible to keep from being sent to Plaszow. When the ghetto was liquidated, he remained as the doctor of the OD "downstairs." By a happy coincidence, he received—as I mentioned before—Hungarian papers for himself and his family. Unfortunately, he did not utilize them in time.

The next day the apartments of those who were murdered were emptied and their personal belongings seized. I asked Kunde, who appeared in the pharmacy, about the fate of the OD men. He answered deliberately and in measured words: "They all went to America for an exchange. Please report this to your personnel."

Insistently, I asked again, "And Dr. Armer went with them as well?"—"The same," he answered. "Did they take their things?" I queried further. After all, I saw their full valises being carried out. Once more he said: "They went together with their personal belongings."

Now I no longer had any doubt about their fate. After several days, I heard talk that they were all shot in the camp in Plaszow and cremated on a pyre. The remainder of the Jews in the service of the Gestapo met a similar fate.

A few days after the liquidation of the OD, all the warehouses on the site of the former ghetto were transferred to Plaszow. The barbed wire, which was the last remaining symbol of the ghetto, was torn down and the renovation of the destroyed buildings started. They were to be made available to the Polish people who were evicted from the officers' colony. Weeks later, the demolition of the walls which surrounded the ghetto began. In this way, all traces (with the exception of two small parts of a wall) were removed from the little town which had experienced such monstrosities.

A new era began. The ghetto was gone. The war was over. People scattered to all parts of the world, but in spite of all the passing years, our friendships with those with whom we lived together through the tragic times and the all too brief moments of elation did not diminish.

A little poem was written about the pharmacy "Under the Eagle," the place where my coworkers and I witnessed the short tragic history of the Cracow ghetto from beginning to end. The poet was Ignacy Nikorowicz, a journalist and author of dramatic plays. He was the son of the composer of the popular chorale, *Z Dymem Pozarow* (With Smoke of Conflagrations).

"Under the Eagle"
The Pharmacy in the Cracow Ghetto

You say sir,
that this pharmacy in the Ghetto,
"Under the Eagle,"
was unique?
That there was none like it
in the entire world?

A strange statement!
Pharmacies are all alike.
They have the same drugs—
there are no differences.

You are mistaken.
It is not so!
Others battle bacteria—
"Under the Eagle"
battled SS men!

This enemy was more deadly,
more violent than microbes.
It must be fought secretly—
carefully, cunningly—
at great risk of death.

Life for hundreds of victims
of those barbaric criminals
was saved
in this pharmacy.

Praise must be sung
for "Under the Eagle,"
this unique pharmacy
in the Ghetto
of Cracow.

A tombstone in remembrance of the deaths in the Plaszow concentration camp

Aktion	German roundups for deportations to concentration camps or immediate mass killings
Arbeitsamt	Work assignment bureau
Arbeitsdienst	Workforce usually made up of prisoners
Emailfabrik	Enamel factory
Herrenvolk	Master race—the "Aryan" people
Judenrat	The Jewish administrative authority appointed by the Germans in Jewish ghettos
Judenrein	"Free of Jews"
Kabala	Jewish school of mysticism and mystical writings
Kennkarten	Identification papers
Krakauer Zeitung	Official German-language newspaper of German General Government
Magister	Master (title)
Oberscharführer	Sergeant-Major of SS
Säuberungskolonne	"Cleaning column"—clean-up squad; part of Sonderkommando units; literally cleaned up after massacres
Shabbes	Jewish Sabbath
Sonderdienst	Auxiliary police units made up of ethnic Germans organized to help the SS
Stimmungs-Berichte	Morale report—sent from the front and occupied areas to Berlin covering all areas from soldiers' morale to state of mind of occupied civilians
Sturmscharführer Kriminalsekretär	Captain of the Gestapo; headed investigative part of SS
Talmud	Body of Jewish law
Talmud Torah	Jewish religious school

Printed in the USA
CPSIA information can be obtained
at www.ICGtesting.com
CBHW020725151124
17218CB00009B/4

9 780896 040878